Marketing Led – Sales Driven

How Successful Businesses Use The Power Of Marketing Plans And Sales Execution To Win In The Marketplace

Ajay K. Sirsi, PhD

Trafford Publishing
www.trafford.com

Order this book online at www.trafford.com
or email orders@trafford.com

Most Trafford titles are also available at major online book retailers.

To Tammara and Belvedere ~ A.S.

Printed in the United States of America.

ISBN: 978-1-4120-2178-4 (sc)
ISBN: 978-1-4122-2135-1 (e)

Trafford rev. 03/11/2014

 www.trafford.com

North America & international
toll-free: 1 888 232 4444 (USA & Canada)
fax: 812 355 4082

Brief Contents

Contents

Overall Plan of the Book

Behind every successful business is the *implementation* of a *superior* strategy

Success in the competitive world of business is not accidental. Successful businesses, from a small home-based entrepreneur to multinational corporations, succeed primarily because they *develop* and *implement superior* business strategies. In other words, they *earn* their success.

In this book I show you how to first develop strategic Marketing Plans. Marketing Plans are implemented in the marketplace by developing Sales and Key Account (Customer) Plans. It is in this way that Marketing and Sales, working together, create value for the customer and win in the marketplace. This is shown in the exhibit below.

- The Marketing Plan outlines segment and customer strategies we want to pursue next year.
- The Marketing Plan is translated into a Sales Plan, which provides the foundation for the development of Key Account (Customer) Plans. It is these plans that get implemented in the marketplace.
- The Sales function meets internally monthly to assess implementation progress and update the rest of the organization.
- Quarterly meetings between Sales, Marketing and other Functions ensures that everyone is working together to develop and implement superior strategies.

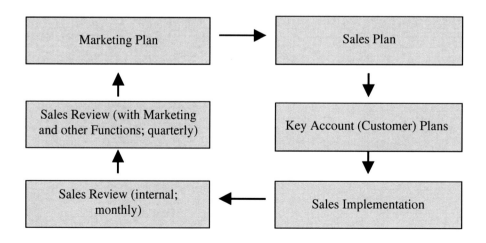

Chapter	Contents
Chapter 1: Why and How Should You Use this Book?	Without the development and implementation of superior strategies, a business cannot succeed.
Chapter 2: The Role of Marketing and Sales in Winning Businesses	Marketing and Sales are two sides of the same coin. They have to work together to understand-create-deliver-manage customer value.
Chapter 3: A Template for Developing Superior Marketing Plans	A clear, easy-to-use, template that enables you to develop superior Marketing Plans.
Chapter 4: Marketing Plans: An Owner's Manual for the Template	Detailed instructions on how to use the Marketing Plan template.
Chapter 5: Avoiding Common Pitfalls in Developing Marketing Plans	Some do's and don'ts to help you develop strategic, actionable Marketing Plans.
Chapter 6: Marketing Planning to Sales Execution: Sales and Key Account (Customer) Plans	Detailed templates that will help you develop Sales and Key Account (Customer) Plans.
Chapter 7: An Annual Planning Calendar For Achieving Cross-Functional Alignment	A detailed annual planning calendar to help you align all your functions so they work together to develop and implement superior strategies. Without this, functions tend to operate in silos.
Appendix 1: Marketing Plan Example	Actual Marketing Plan to help you develop your superior plan.
Appendix 2: Sales Plan Example	Sales Plans provide the direction for the development of Key Account (Customer) Plans. This detailed example shows you how.
Appendix 3: Key Account (Customer) Plan Example	This is where the rubber meets the road. A detailed example to guide your Customer plans.
Glossary	A list of terms for quick and easy reference.

Acknowledgements

In my professional life, I have the luxury of reading, thinking, writing and teaching at the University. However, without the ability to apply my thoughts in business organizations throughout the world, my messages would be less than compelling.

I, therefore, wish to thank the numerous business leaders with whom I have worked in a consulting capacity. Without them, I could not learn.

This book was my sabbatical project. Thank you, York University and the Schulich School of Business, for giving me the time off to work, think, write and grow.

Carole Tanaka patiently worked with me to format the manuscript. Many a time I called her to cancel our work session because I had not progressed in my writing. She never once complained. Thank you, Carole.

My parents have always cheered my writing efforts. I thank them for their encouragement.

This book is dedicated to my wife, Tammara. Writing is a lonely journey, but she has been my constant companion, content to wait for me to emerge from my study after hours of work on the book. I could not do what I do without her love, support and help. She is my inspiration.

This book is also dedicated to Belvedere, our poodle. The name of the customer on the Key Account Plan, Belvedere Widget Inc., is for her. With her playfulness, sense of humor and nobility, she has brought great joy into our lives.

Ajay K. Sirsi, PhD
asirsi@schulich.yorku.ca

About the Author

Ajay K. Sirsi, **PhD**, is a Marketing Professor at the Schulich School of Business, York University, Toronto, Canada, where he teaches Strategic Market Planning, Marketing Research, and Marketing Management. He teaches executive management classes in Brand Equity, Marketing Management, and Marketing Strategy and Sales Planning in the Executive Development Program at York University. He also teaches Marketing Research and Marketing Management for the Professional Marketing Research Society (PMRS). Ajay has an extensive consulting practice in which he works with business executives on a range of marketing and sales issues.

His current research focuses on creating customer value, developing strategic marketing plans and sales execution, sales force effectiveness, managerial effectiveness, and physician decision making.

Prof. Sirsi is the author of many articles which have appeared in prominent academic and practitioner journals such as the *Journal of Consumer Research*, *Canadian Journal of Marketing Research*, the *Journal of Health Care Marketing*, the *Journal of Hospital Marketing*, and the *Journal of Professional Services Marketing*. He is a recipient of the prestigious Robert Ferber Award and the award for best article published in the *Journal of Consumer Research*.

Ajay has undertaken both **consulting** and **educational activities** for FT Global 500 corporations in the United States, Canada, Brazil, China, France, India, Japan and Korea in the areas of developing business and marketing strategy, sales execution, developing and implementing customer value, building brand identity/equity, building corporate brands, building differentiation strategies, customer needs assessment, customer satisfaction and service quality, strategic planning for services, new product development, segmentation and product positioning, and sales training.

His clients include Bayer, Bombardier, Glaxo SmithKline, Imperial Oil, International Paper, Manulife Financial, Novartis, Royal Bank, and TELUS.

Chapter 1

Why And How Should *You* Use This Book?

In This Chapter You Will Find...

➢ The reasons why you should develop and implement plans in your business

➢ Why Marketing and Sales should work together to create customer value and win in the marketplace

➢ Why, in some businesses, Marketing and Sales do not work well together

➢ The annual planning process used by successful businesses to develop Marketing Plans and implement these plans by developing Sales and Key Account (Customer) Plans

➢ What happens when a business does not put in place a mechanism for Marketing and Sales to work together

➢ Some myths about the planning effort
   ➢ Myth 1: Planning has to be cumbersome
   ➢ Myth 2: Developing plans takes up precious time that could have been spent in running the business
   ➢ Myth 3: "Our business is not yet ready to think strategically."
   ➢ Myth 4: The Marketing Plan is only relevant to the Marketing function

➢ A broad outline on how to use this book

➢ Short vignettes of three businesses and how they can use the concepts and tools in this book

Behind Every Successful Business Is the *Implementation* Of A *Superior Strategy*

Success in the competitive world of business is not accidental. Successful businesses, from a small home-based entrepreneur to multinational corporations, succeed primarily because they *develop and implement superior business strategies.* In other words, these businesses *earn* their success.

Although there are many definitions of the word "strategy", think of strategy as a plan that you formulate to win in the marketplace.

So, whether you are a budding entrepreneur embarking on a nascent business venture or the vice president of a business division, your success will primarily depend upon your ability to *formulate* and *execute* a superior plan for your business. Business history teaches us that organizations that fail in the marketplace, fail primarily because they do not formulate a superior plan, or strategy.

That is the reason you need to read and implement the concepts and tools in this book – the future of your business depends on it.

This book is written in a way that is accessible to all business people, regardless of formal training. I have distilled, within the pages contained in this book, years of experience working with large and small business organizations helping them develop and implement successful plans.

There are no guarantees in business, one only gets the chance to act. However, I can promise you that if you follow the Marketing and Sales discipline outlined in this book, your odds of succeeding will improve.

The Power Of Marketing And Sales Partnership

Notice that in the preceding paragraphs I said that your success will primarily depend upon your ability to *formulate* and *execute* a superior plan for your business. How is this done in reality? It is achieved by first developing a strategic Marketing Plan and then *translating* it into Sales and Key Account (Customer) Plans[1] that are implemented. When this is achieved, Marketing and Sales work in partnership to achieve business success.

Unfortunately, in many organizations Marketing and Sales do not work well together. In fact, in some businesses I have worked with, their relationship is downright hostile. If not hostile, they tolerate each other. The following comment made to me by a senior manager at a large multinational is emblematic:

> **"In our business we develop long-term [Marketing] plans dutifully each year, but we do not act on them. Sales throws them away and does day-to-day tactical things."**

There are three key reasons for the above situation:

1. The role of Marketing and Sales is not clearly defined. How about in your business? Can you answer honestly that everyone in your organization knows the unique contribution made by Marketing and Sales? In my experience, in many organizations the roles are fuzzy.

2. There is no mechanism in place to develop the required partnership between Marketing and the Sales function. This situation is in large part a consequence of the fuzzy role definitions. Marketing and Sales partnerships are essential and powerful. This is done by first developing Marketing Plans and then *translating* them into actionable Sales and Key Account (Customer) Plans.

---

[1] I am going to use the terms Key Account and Customer Plans interchangeably. A Key Account Plan *is* a Customer Plan developed for a key customer.

This is what happens if there is no mechanism for Marketing and Sales to work together:

"Marketing hands us a plan and says, 'Go and implement this plan.' Sales does not act on this because they feel *they* own the customer. But, Marketing says *they* own the customer."

The above comment was made to me by the Vice President in charge of Sales at a client organization.

Marketing and Sales are part of the same system – Identifying, Satisfying and Keeping customers.

They need each other, the total task cannot be completed until they work together as one team.

3.   There is no mechanism to jointly review Sales execution in the field to learn and make changes for the following year. Although this point may seem obvious, it is an important one. Marketing and Sales have to jointly review the business' strategies and field implementation to learn from successes and failures and use this learning to make any necessary changes for the next planning cycle.

Therefore, the blueprint for success is the framework I have depicted in Exhibit 1.1.

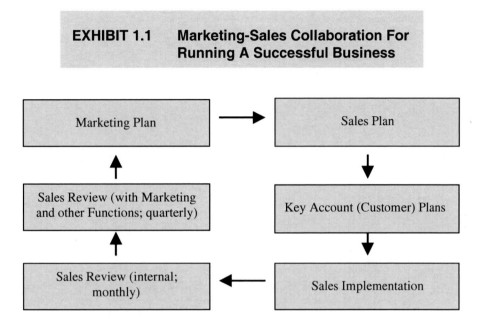

EXHIBIT 1.1   Marketing-Sales Collaboration For Running A Successful Business

As you can see from Exhibit 1.1, a business starts by developing a yearly Marketing Plan, which contains details on segments, customers, competitors and marketing strategies to achieve certain business objectives. Essentially, the role of the Marketing Plan is "context setting" for the rest of the business. However, a Marketing Plan is not an implementable document. If you gave it to a sales person and asked him or her to implement it, this professional would not know what to do with it (and, rightly so). Therefore, the Marketing Plan needs to be translated into Sales and Key Account (Customer) Plans. Now, *these* are highly implementable documents indeed.

The Sales function implements these plans in the field and meets internally monthly to review execution and update the rest of the organization. Then, both Marketing and Sales (along with other functions) conduct a Sales Review every quarter to assess what went right and what went wrong, and the process starts all over again next year.

The process you see in Exhibit 1.1 is for a planning cycle of one year.

As Exhibit 1.1 demonstrates, the discipline to run a successful business requires the constant interplay between strategy and implementation. Such discipline takes effort to acquire, but without it, a business is never truly successful.

What Happens If You Do Not Follow This Process?

1. Turf wars. Not following the blueprint laid out in Exhibit 1.1 is a guarantee of turf wars. I have encountered businesses where the perennial bone of contention between Marketing and Sales is the answer to the question:

"Who owns the customer in our business?"

Sound familiar? Of course, both functions feel *they* own the customer and the other is in the way. I think this is a waste of time.

2. Flying accusations. Without the process I have outlined, you hear such comments from the Sales organization:

"In our organization, the Marketing function is too theoretical, ivory-tower. They are completely disconnected with Sales. They do not have a concept of the realities of the marketplace. They come up with these fancy marketing schemes that do not work."

Or, you will hear people in Marketing saying such things as:

> **"Our Sales organization is too tactical. There is no strategy behind their efforts. As a result, they are quick to cut price to get the sale. In the long run, this will kill our business."**

3. A drifting business. In my experience, businesses that do not develop and implement superior strategies tend to drift. Some go belly up and end up in the Business Hall of Shame, while others continue to under perform.

Myths About The Planning Effort

Myth #1. Planning has to be cumbersome.

As you will see in this book, I have presented straightforward templates to use in developing strategic Marketing Plans, Sales Plans and Key Account (Customer) Plans. The planning effort does not have to be cumbersome. It does not have to be bureaucratic and full of forms and the like. However, planning has to be formal and you should put your plans down on paper.

Putting your plans down on paper forces you to be disciplined in your thinking and avoids "pie-in-the-sky" type thinking. I read someplace once that discipline leads to freedom. The author is absolutely right. A disciplined approach to your business will go a long way in ensuring your success.

There is another reason why you should develop formal plans and put them down on paper – sharing them with others in your business. A formal plan unifies efforts within an organization. For example, later you will see that a Marketing Plan requires you to identify tactics to implement each Marketing strategy. These tactics specify timelines and person responsibilities and resources required. It is in this way that different members within an organization come to share a common vision and sense of direction.

A plan is like a playbook for a sports team. Without it, one person wants to rush the ball, the other wants to throw a long pass, while the third thinks it is half time!

Myth #2. Developing plans takes up precious time that could have been spent in running the business.

Don't you believe this for a second. A business unit manager once said to me,

> **"I do not have time to waste developing Marketing Plans. I have a business to run."**

Try as I might, I could not convince him otherwise.

If you read between the lines, this is what the manager is *really* saying.

> **"I do not take a strategic view of my business. I am a tactician. I operate on a trial and error basis. I go from putting out one fire to the next. I try something and, if it does not work, I try something else."**

Three years later the business was sold for poor performance and this manager lost his job in the process.

> **In my consulting work I have documented proof that businesses that register superior marketplace performance also develop superior plans.**

Myth #3. Our business is not yet ready to think strategically.

I hear this all the time and it never ceases to amaze me how some businesses lull themselves into a false sense of security. I hear how the business does not have time to think strategically or how the business does not have the resources to develop Marketing Plans.

The reality is this: Developing a Marketing Plan and its implementation should be a business habit, a discipline the business imposes on itself to be proactive in the marketplace.

Excellence is a habit, not an act

The day will never arrive when all your projects are done and you are ready to start thinking strategically. There will always be some excuse holding you back.

So, my advice is this

Start small, but start now.

The first time you develop a Marketing Plan, it may only be a few pages long, and that is all right. The next time your Plan will be improved over the first attempt, and so it will go.

Remember, no business gets planning perfect, there is always something to learn.

I have found that successful businesses always question their business model, never being content to sit on their laurels. They are constantly improving, making small changes that, over time, add up to a significant amount.

If it ain't broke, fix it!

Myth #4. The Marketing Plan is relevant only to the Marketing function.

Nothing could be farther from the truth. In actuality, a Marketing Plan is a document that is at the heart of all planning efforts. If done right (and I will show you how to develop a sound Plan) a Marketing Plan unifies the entire organization's functions.

We have already seen how the Marketing Plan initiates the Sales Plan and Key Account (Customer) Plans. But, as you will see later, the Marketing Plan also initiates other functional plans within a business -- Production Plans, Capital Plans, Human Resource Plans, IT Plans, Supply Chain Plans, etc.

Also, Marketing should not be the sole domain of the Marketing function, it should be everyone's concern within your business. I have always felt that Marketing should be a state of mind within any business. And, if you notice how successful businesses work, it is!

How Should You Use This Book?

This book can be used by any business person, manufacturing a good or providing a service, wanting to outfox competitors and succeed in the marketplace. I have also used the planning templates in this book with government agencies and non-profit organizations (although the templates need to be modified slightly for their needs; however, the basic ideas apply equally to any business).

Let us start with Exhibit 1.1, which is essentially the framework for the chapters in this book. Start your planning process by developing a Marketing Plan using the tools contained in this book.

The Marketing Plan should be developed no later than September 1 for the next year's planning cycle (the last chapter in this book outlines planning timelines and other details).

Although the steward for developing the Marketing Plan is the Marketing function, as you will see (in the last chapter on planning timelines) other functions (most actively

Sales) are also involved in its construction. It is in this way that the entire organization takes ownership of issues relating to customers and markets.

The Marketing Plan is a highly strategic document that cannot be implemented in its current shape. It needs to be translated into such implementation details for the Sales function as:

- What sales targets should we set for our market segments (identified and profiled by the Marketing function)?
- What value propositions should we develop for customers (based on segment value propositions identified by the Marketing function)?
- What piece of this customer's order book should we aim for (based on a profile of the customer's needs and attractiveness done by the Marketing function)?

Therefore, your next step should be to ensure that Marketing and Sales work together (again, I have provided details in the last chapter) to translate the Marketing Plan into Sales and Key Account (Customer) Plans (of course, you will find templates for these plans later in the book).

As you will see when you examine the template to develop a Marketing Plan, it (if done correctly) sets up the development of Sales and Key Account (Customer) Plans. In other words, one plan should seamlessly flow into the other plan.

As you proceed from the Marketing Plan to Sales Plans to Key Account (Customer) Plans, you move from the realm of strategy to the realm of implementation.

Sales and Customer Plans should be finalized by November 1, at the latest. This ensures that other functions (for example, Production) have enough time to gear up their resources for the next year.

How To Use This Book: A Profile Of Three Businesses

Tom is an entrepreneur who runs a cleaning business. Being a one-man show, he is the Marketing and Sales function, all rolled into one. How should he use this book? He should start by developing a Marketing Plan that outlines his key objectives and strategies for the next year. He should then translate this document into a combined Sales/Customer Plan[2], depending upon the scope of his business.

Ron is a partner in a small business that supplies food products to other businesses such as retailers and institutions (e.g., hospitals). He looks after the Marketing function, while his partner, Susan, looks after the Sales function. They have 10 sales professionals working for them. They have divided their market into 5 districts; each district is served by two salespeople.

Ron wants to advertise on TV, but Susan feels it is too expensive and probably will not be very effective. Ron wishes Susan's Monday-morning Sales meetings were more like Sales meetings, rather than trial and error sessions.

Ron and Susan have a large enough business, so they should develop a Marketing Plan for the next year, a Sales Plan by district and Customer Plans for their key customers. Doing this will enable them to make informed decisions about such issues as whether TV advertising is the best option, or what targeted approach a sales professional should take to generate new accounts.

Vicki is the senior vice president of a division that makes specialty paper. Her division is part of a large multinational, with operations in 50 countries. Vicki's division makes high-end paper for such applications as photo printing, labels, and forms. Each product line is unique. Vicki would develop a Marketing Plan for her overall business, as well as individual Marketing Plans for each product line. She would also work with the Sales function to develop Sales and Key Account (Customer) Plans.

Many businesses flounder because they lack a disciplined approach to their business. The process outlined in Exhibit 1.1 is essentially such a discipline.

---

[2] As we will see later, a Customer Plan can be developed for one customer, or it can encompass thousands of customers (e.g., the Small Office Home Office customer segment).

Chapter 2

The Role of Marketing and Sales in Winning Businesses

In This Chapter You Will Find...

- ➤ The four things successful businesses do well:
  - ➤ Understand customer needs
  - ➤ Create customer value
  - ➤ Deliver customer value
  - ➤ Manage customer value

- ➤ The role of Marketing and Sales in the understand-create-deliver-manage customer value cycle

- ➤ Details on understanding customer needs
  - ➤ How to segment markets and customers
  - ➤ Market segmentation example
  - ➤ Market segmentation pitfalls

- ➤ Details on creating, delivering and managing customer value
  - ➤ Segment-specific value propositions
  - ➤ Customer-specific value propositions

- ➤ Implementing Sales and Customer Plans and making changes

All successful businesses do four things well. They:

> • Understand customer needs
> • Create value for chosen customers (their target markets)
> • Deliver customer value
> • Manage customer value

This is shown in Exhibit 2.1.

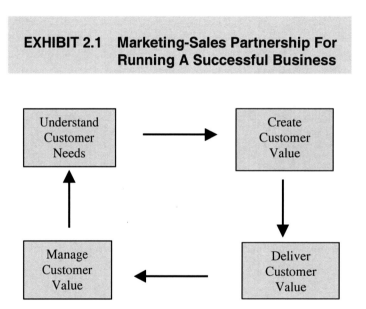

EXHIBIT 2.1   Marketing-Sales Partnership For Running A Successful Business

Marketing and Sales have different, but complementary, roles to play in the understand-create-deliver-manage customer value cycle as shown in Exhibit 2.2.

EXHIBIT 2.2   The Role Of Marketing And Sales In Successful Businesses

	Understand Customer Needs	Create Customer Value	Deliver Customer Value	Manage Customer Value
Role of Marketing	• Conduct formal marketing research • Customer visits • Market segmentation matrix • Competitive analysis • Measure segment, customer and product attractiveness	• Develop Marketing Plan • Develop segment specific value propositions (in Marketing Plan) • Pricing strategy and tactics	• Accompany Sales on periodic sales calls	• Annual customer satisfaction measurement • Sharing customer satisfaction results with key decision makers • Customer communication • Marketing effectiveness goals3 • Influence all departments and employees to be customer centered • Conduct sales review jointly with Sales • Segment, customer, product mix review • Brand management

_____

[3] Includes target segment share and target segment return on investment (ROI)

	Understand Customer Needs	**Create Customer Value**	**Deliver Customer Value**	**Manage Customer Value**
Role of Sales	• Sales calls • Develop specialized knowledge of customer's industry and business	• Develop Sales Plans • Develop Key Account (Customer) Plans • Develop customer specific value propositions (in Customer Plans)	• Customer value proposition delivery (including service level agreements4)	• Participate in customer satisfaction measurement • Feedback customer needs and ideas to product development • Sales effectiveness goals5 • Conduct sales review jointly with Marketing • Get paid for value being delivered to customer • Manage customer relationships for long term profitability

---

[4] Service Level Agreements (SLAs) are previously agreed-to customer commitments such as volume, product specifications, delivery schedules, invoicing, etc.
[5] Includes target customer sales volumes and target customer ROI

Understand Customer Needs

Without an accurate understanding of customer needs it is not possible to develop winning strategies in the marketplace. This is a known fact. Typically, however, we tend to assume that the job of gathering insight into customers' needs falls into Marketing's lap, and we leave it at that.

Nothing could be further from the truth.

The truth is this: The Sales function in an organization has knowledge about the customer that typically does not get utilized.

Therefore, as shown in Exhibit 2.2, Marketing should conduct formal marketing research studies and participate in sales visits, while Sales should develop a specialized knowledge about the customer's industry and business.

In Chapter 7, I will show you how to use the specialized knowledge gathered by Sales in the process of formulating Marketing Plans. Without this, the valuable data gathered by Sales goes to waste.

At the end of the Understand Customer Needs phase your business should have segmented your markets and customers. I turn to this topic next.

A Primer On Market Segmentation

Market segmentation is a fundamental strategic activity conducted by a business. The truth is that most businesses do not appreciate the full meaning of this concept, nor do they know exactly how to implement it as they run their business day-to-day.

Segmentation remains a "fuzzy" area that proves most troublesome to a business. We think we understand what it is and why we segment markets, but in reality, even the most sophisticated marketing professionals are sometimes flustered by this concept.

There are *three* key tenets of market segmentation. These are:

> Key Tenets Of Market Segmentation
>
> - A business exists to be profitable.
> - All customers are not created equal.
> - We cannot be all things to all customers.

A business exists to be profitable

Few people would have a problem with this statement. Yet, most businesses do not appreciate the fact that, in order to be profitable, they have to take a cold, hard look at their marketplace and recognize differential profitable opportunities among customers.

I use the word "profitable" as a synonym for "effective". In other words, even if you are a non-profit organization, you need to be effective (although you may not make a "profit"). And, as I will argue, you cannot be effective unless you segment your markets.

All customers are not created equal

In order to be profitable, the concept of market segmentation maintains that a business has to come to the recognition that there are two variables that differentiate customers – their *needs* and their *propensity (willingness) to pay* for our value creation efforts.

Therefore, all customers are not created equal and we should not treat them that way. The truth is that some customer needs (market segments) are more attractive than others. Not recognizing this fact leads to trouble for a business.

We cannot be all things to all customers

A corollary to the above fact is that a business cannot serve all customer needs. Therefore, every business has to ask and answer two strategic questions:

- Which needs (segments) do we want to serve?
- How do we want to serve those needs?

In other words, a business has to choose which market segments it wants to serve (target markets) and then tailor its marketing strategies and tactics to serve the chosen segment.

A fundamental mistake made by many businesses is to try to be all things to all customers. The last time this approach worked was when Henry Ford said his customers could have any car they wanted – as long as it was a Model T and it was black in color. Of course, that was before Ford's customers had alternatives.

The rush to be all things to all customers masks the fact that customers differ in their attractiveness. Some customers are costlier to serve than others, and yet are only willing to pay the same invoice price. The concept of market segmentation forces a business to be critical in choosing which customer needs (segments) it should serve. This discipline enables the business to stay on the path to profitability.

> **The bottom line is this – businesses that want to be profitable have no choice, they must segment their markets.**

Market Segmentation Defined

A market segment is a group of customers with the following characteristics:

> A Market Segment is…
>
> ➢ A group of customers with a distinct set of needs and propensities to pay.
> ➢ Whose needs demand a distinct set of marketing strategies in order to be satisfied.
> ➢ The needs of the segment are different from the needs of another segment.

An excellent example of market segmentation may be found in Exhibit 2.3.

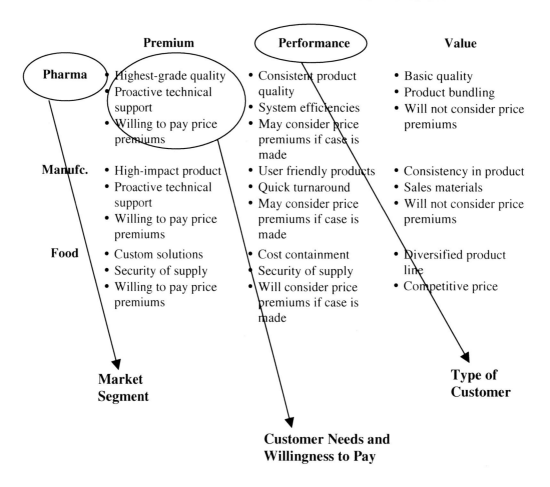

EXHIBIT 2.3   Market Segmentation Example

	Premium	Performance	Value
Pharma	• Highest-grade quality • Proactive technical support • Willing to pay price premiums	• Consistent product quality • System efficiencies • May consider price premiums if case is made	• Basic quality • Product bundling • Will not consider price premiums
Manufc.	• High-impact product • Proactive technical support • Willing to pay price premiums	• User friendly products • Quick turnaround • May consider price premiums if case is made	• Consistency in product • Sales materials • Will not consider price premiums
Food	• Custom solutions • Security of supply • Willing to pay price premiums	• Cost containment • Security of supply • Will consider price premiums if case is made	• Diversified product line • Competitive price

Market Segment

Customer Needs and Willingness to Pay

Type of Customer

Exhibit 2.3 reveals a market by customer segment grid. In the example (simplified from one of my consulting projects) this business supplies raw materials to three market segments – pharmaceutical firms, manufacturing firms and food service firms. Further, the business has recognized three customer types within these segments – Premium, Performance and Value customers[6].

Each cell in the matrix outlines the customer's needs and price sensitivity, thus revealing how attractive the customer is to us. *Such a grid is invaluable because it enables us to start thinking about what value to create for each customer segment.*

As can be seen from the Exhibit, Premium customers demand better goods and services, but are also willing to pay. Performance customers are willing to listen to our value creation efforts, but Value customers just want a basic product (goods and services) at a basic price. The concept of market segmentation says that, while we may choose to serve all these customer types, we cannot serve them in the same way (if we did we would not be profitable).

The process of segmentation is:

> Identify market segments according to some criteria (discussed below).
> Choose segments you want to serve.
> Tailor your marketing mix elements (product strategy, pricing strategy, channel of distribution strategy, marketing communications strategy) to best serve the chosen segment(s).

How To Segment Markets

The best way to segment markets is to examine customer needs and group those needs in some meaningful fashion. For example, a lumber business may decide to segment its customers into three "need groups". These could be:

* Do-it-yourself segment.
* Industrial segment (for example, pallet manufacturers).
* Home building segment.

---

[6] The categorization of customers into Premium, Performance, and Value is arbitrary; you may choose other names and criteria to classify your customers.

Why did this business choose these segments? First, each of these segments represents a distinct group of customers with a distinct set of needs that need to be served in a distinct way, different from the other groups. For example, the needs of a do-it-yourselfer buying wood to remodel his deck at home are different from a large builder of tract homes, and therefore, each need (segment) has to be served differently.

Second, the business has decided that serving these market segments represents the best path to profitability, over other segments it could have served (for example, the furniture manufacturing segment).

Market Segmentation Pitfalls

Using demographic segmentation

As stated earlier, a business should segment its markets using two criteria: (1) customer needs and (2) customer attractiveness.

One common pitfall in market segmentation is to segment customers according to demographic criteria such as size, geography, sales, or SIC codes (in business-to-business markets), or such criteria as income or age (in business-to-consumer markets). While this is an easy way to segment markets, it is not the most effective because demographic variables do not differentiate between customer needs. So, it is possible that two different "segments" based, say, on firm size or income, may actually have similar needs.

Segmenting by product

A mistake made by some businesses is to segment their markets by product and not by need. Typically, these businesses look at their existing product lines and then identify need groups as those customers who buy product line 1, those that buy product line 2, and so on.

For example, the lumber business above may segment its markets into lumber customers and plywood customers. What is the danger in this? It ignores the overlapping needs customers may have. It assumes that purchasers of plywood have no need for lumber. Therefore, the business cannot take a holistic look at its product mix.

Using complex segmentation schemes that are not actionable

One compelling reason why a business should segment its markets is so that it allocates its resources for maximum impact. This only happens when everyone within the business clearly understands what segments are strategic and what role they play in serving the chosen market segments.

Complex segmentation schemes collapse under their own weight. Consider this example: After segmenting by product lines a business further segments its markets using multiple variables including geography, customer need and customer business type. The resulting scheme is so cumbersome that it is completely non-actionable. Frustrated, the business then abandons segmenting its markets completely.

My good friend and business colleague, Craig Wilson, has this to say about market segmentation:

> **"It is a travesty that the consulting and academic worlds have made market segmentation complex, difficult and cumbersome, when in reality, market segmentation is common sense, simple and powerful."**

So, the recommendation is clear – use *simple* ways to segment your markets and communicate to the rest of your organization the strategic significance of the chosen market segments.

Using the same segmentation scheme as our competitors

Ultimately, a business' chosen segmentation scheme should provide it with a competitive advantage in the marketplace by enabling it to serve customer needs in a superior way to its competitors.

Michael Dell's (founder of Dell computers) success resulted in part because he was astute enough to recognize that there was a better way to serve latent customer needs. He segmented the market according to what channels of distribution competitors were using to serve customers.

Before him, all competitors used the same method to serve customers – through retailers. Dell revolutionized the industry by recognizing an unmet customer need (a segment) – customers who could be served directly from the manufacturer.

The lesson is clear – do not merely imitate your competitors' segmentation schemes. Find alternate ways of segmenting your markets that can yield competitive difference and advantage.

Being constrained by the current situation

Managers are not paid to make the obvious happen (or not happen). When thinking about market segments a pitfall to avoid is to be constrained by current situations such as capacity or other ability to serve.

Employ a two-step approach. Initially, segment your markets without consideration of any organizational constraints. Then, impose business constraints upon the market segments to make decisions on which segments you can serve well. There is an added advantage of this exercise – it will reveal to you what resources you may need to invest in to take full advantage of your segmentation scheme.

Not investing in emerging segments

A concept called "disruptive technologies" torpedoes many businesses over time. Self serve photocopiers were a disruptive technology that eliminated the need to have a central photocopy department in business organizations. Yet, central photocopy departments ignored self-serve copiers, viewing them as a temporary phenomenon that would disappear.

Similarly, every business should spend some of its marketing effort into identifying and targeting emerging segments. IBM nearly went under because of its initial failure to identify the emerging segment of consumers that needed desktop computing power.

Some businesses consider new and emerging segments as a nuisance to their on-going business instead of viewing them as opportunities to create a sustainable competitive advantage. Do not fall into this trap.

Forgetting that segments change over time

Every business should keep two factors paramount as it periodically evaluates a market segment: (1) Are segment needs changing, and if so, how? and (2) Does the segment continue to be attractive for us to serve?

It is wise to remember that a customer-focused business should not only be concerned about creating customer value from market segmentation analysis, but also be focused about capturing some of the created value for itself through periodic analysis of segment attractiveness.

Use the checklist below to evaluate your segmentation efforts.

EXHIBIT 2.4   Market Segmentation Checklist

You must answer "Yes" to all questions	Yes	No
1. Is our segmentation scheme simple?	☐	☐
2. Will people understand and use it?	☐	☐
3. Have we segmented our markets and customers using existing data (are we starting small, but starting now)?	☐	☐
4. Have we utilized customer needs and attractiveness in our segmentation?	☐	☐
5. Is our segmentation scheme actionable (can we actually implement this)?	☐	☐
6. Will our segmentation scheme give us a competitive advantage (or, is our segmentation the same as our competitors')?	☐	☐
7. Do we have the means to evolve our segmentation scheme over time?	☐	☐

The process of market segmentation enables us to **Understand**, **Create**, **Deliver** and **Manage** customer value by imposing a discipline on businesses to (1) identify customer needs and define market segments, (2) choose market segments, (3) serve market segments, and (4) periodically analyze segments to identify changing needs and profitability patterns.

Create Customer Value

As shown in Exhibit 2.2, the output of the Understand Customer Needs phase is a matrix on market segmentation. In the Create Customer Value phase the business organization offers goods and services to satisfy the needs of its customers. Both Marketing and Sales have a role to play here.

Marketing develops segment-specific value propositions (described in the Marketing Plan) and Sales develops customer-specific value propositions (described in Key Account or Customer Plans).

In Exhibit 2.5 you will find an example of segment-specific value propositions. Exhibit 2.6 shows an example of customer-specific value propositions.

EXHIBIT 2.5   Segment-Specific Value Propositions[7]

	Premium	Performance	Value
Pharma	• Grade A product • Superior product performance • Continuous availability • Dedicated Technical Service Team	• Product quality guarantees • High quality control standards • Aesthetic packages • Dedicated Technical Service Team	• Grade B Product • Technical Team available as requested
Manufc.	• Grade AA Product • Superior product performance • Inventory Management • Dedicated Technical Service Team	• User friendly products that reduce costs • Quick turnaround • Ability to do short product runs	• Grade BB product • Consistency in product • Sales materials • Technical Team available at extra charge
Food	• Grade A Product • Custom Solutions Team • Dedicated Sales Team	• Cost containment • Security of supply • Value creation for end consumer	• Diversified product line • Competitive price

---

[7] Appendix 2 (Sales Plan example) provides more details on this topic.

EXHIBIT 2.6   Tam-Tam Inc. Customer Specific Value Propositions[8]

General Customer Description

Tam-Tam Inc. is a Premium customer in the Pharmaceutical market segment. They manufacture high-end lotions and creams for brand-name cosmetics companies that are sold through department stores and a select number of drug stores.

Customer Needs
- Tam-Tam Inc. products are all high-end. They rely on visual appeal in the store for sales. As such, the package needs to be very attractive. Therefore, our packaging solutions have to support high-end graphics applications.
- Tam-Tam Inc. is a Premium customer. They are relatively price insensitive because their primary needs have to do with a high-grade product, consistent product quality, reliability of supply and proactive technical support.

Customer Value Propositions

We will retain this attractive customer by offering these value propositions:

- Grade A product quality.
- High brightness product.
- Product availability guarantees.
- Superior graphics capability.
- Proactive technical support team.
- Dedicated sales team.
- Inventory management.

Deliver Customer Value

At this stage the Sales function swings into full gear and delivers the value that has been created for customers as outlined in the Sales Plan and Key Account (Customer) Plans. The Marketing function can play an important role here by periodically

---

[8] In Appendix 3 I provide a Key Account (Customer) Plan that discusses this topic in great detail.

accompanying Sales on customer visits to get a first-hand impression of how receptive customers are to our goods and services.

Manage Customer Value

As you can see from Exhibit 2.2, this phase is like the rudder on a boat, it enables us to constantly make adjustments to our strategies and tactics.

The Marketing function should do the following in this phase:

➢ Measure customer satisfaction annually to understand customers' satisfaction with our goods and services.
➢ Share customer satisfaction data with key decision-makers to make adjustments in strategies and tactics.
➢ Go beyond customer satisfaction and delve deeper into causes of customer satisfaction, dissatisfaction and defection.
➢ Set Marketing effectiveness goals such as target segment share and target segment return on investment. Communicate Marketing effectiveness within business.
➢ Educate all functional areas within the business on their role in being a customer-centric organization.
➢ Review the attractiveness of segments, customers and products to ensure business is serving the right segments and customers with the right mix of goods and services.[9]
➢ Manage the transition of products to brand status and maintain long-term health of brands.
➢ Review sales execution in the field by conducting a sales review, jointly with Sales. This is a critical step because it will reveal potential problem areas to be corrected for the next year. In other words, if the organization's sales performance in the field does not measure up to expectations the problem could lie in three areas: (1) Marketing did not do a good enough job of forecasting demand; (2) Sales did not do a good enough job in executing via Sales and Customer Plans; (3) An individual salesperson needs additional training to perform better.

---

[9] Every year a business should routinely evaluate three things: segments it operates in, customers it serves, and the mix of goods and services it serves customers with. Therefore, this analysis should reveal which segments the business should pursue and which segments it should exit. The analysis should also reveal which customers need to be "fired" (the best run businesses I know let go of their most unattractive customers on an annual basis). They do this based on developing customer scorecards, which contain such metrics as sales (both absolute sales and percentage of customer's total order book), profits, cost to serve customer, strategic fit with business, loyalty, etc.

In this phase, the role of the Sales function is:

➢ Participate in customer satisfaction measurement.
➢ Provide feedback on customer needs and new ideas to Marketing.
➢ Set sales effectiveness goals such as target customer sales volumes and target customer return on investment.
➢ Communicate sales effectiveness goals within organization.
➢ Manage customer relationships for long-term profitability.
➢ Conduct sales review, jointly with Marketing.

Chapter 3

A Template For Developing Superior Marketing Plans

In This Chapter You Will Find...

➢ How successful businesses achieve inter-functional alignment by developing and linking these plans:
    ➢ Strategic Plan
    ➢ Marketing Plan
    ➢ Sales and Key Account (Customer) Plans
    ➢ Functional Plans: Production, Finance, HR, IT, etc.

➢ The key differences between a Strategic Plan and a Marketing Plan

➢ How a Marketing Plan enables you to increase the odds for success

➢ An easy-to-use template to develop strategic Marketing Plans
    ➢ Executive summary
    ➢ Table of contents
    ➢ Marketplace analysis
    ➢ Competitive analysis
    ➢ Segmentation analysis: Markets and customers
    ➢ SWOT analysis
    ➢ Identification of key issues facing your business
    ➢ Setting segment objectives
    ➢ Marketing strategies and tactics
    ➢ Positioning relative to the competition
    ➢ Marketing – Sales linkage
    ➢ Key business outcomes
    ➢ Marketing Plan budget
    ➢ Marketing Plan control
    ➢ Appendix

A singular trait of a forward-thinking, customer-focused business is *enterprise alignment*. In these businesses, all functions, regardless of what they do, focus on understanding-creating-delivering-managing customer value. Without an aligned enterprise you often come across such situations (all examples from my consulting work):

- Marketing develops Marketing Plans and hands them over to the Sales function, which promptly ignores them and proceeds to execute tactical sales initiatives.
- The Sales function makes promises to customers that Production cannot meet. One manager told me, "Last year, we sold more than our capacity." (Say, the business can make 100 widgets annually, the sales force sold 125 widgets.) How is this possible? It happens because the two functions are operating in silos, and therefore, do not talk with each other. The sales force has made promises to customers that cannot be kept.
- The HR function is frustrated because nobody invites them to strategy sessions. Instead, the HR function is treated as an administrative function that hires, motivates and fires individuals.
- In spite of the Marketing function saying that the customer wants 10-inch widgets, the factory produces 12-inch widgets. Why? This is because the Production manager is measured and compensated on how efficiently the factory runs, not on how customer-focused he is. Senior management may talk about the need to be customer-focused, but unless metrics are aligned with customer needs, such talk will only remain in the realm of rhetoric.

How do customer-focused firms achieve enterprise alignment? They do this with their annual planning process depicted in **Exhibit 3.1** (shown below).

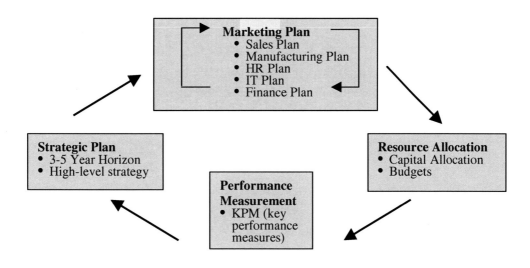

As you can see from the Exhibit, it starts with the development of a Strategic Plan for the business. The Strategic Plan is normally developed for a 3 – 5 year time horizon and it outlines the overall corporate direction. Therefore, strategies are set at a very high level to outline such issues as what markets the corporation will serve, how much capital will be required, what goods and services the corporation will make, etc.

The ultimate test of any business' success is determined by the superiority of its strategies and tactics at the *customer* level. However, the Strategic Plan is a document that cannot be implemented in its current form at the customer level. If you gave your business' Strategic Plan to a sales person and asked her to implement it, she would rightly look askance. She would not know what to do with it.

For this reason, we develop one-year increments of the Strategic Plan. This plan is called the Marketing Plan. Think of the Strategic Plan as a loaf of bread and the Marketing Plan as a slice.

There are two key differences between a Strategic Plan and a Marketing Plan

➤ **Time horizon.** A Strategic Plan is normally developed for a 3 – 5 year time horizon, while a Marketing Plan is developed for a period of 1 year.

➤ **Level of detail.** A Marketing Plan contains the same kinds of analyses as in the Strategic Plan (evaluation of markets, customers, competitors, etc.), but, in addition, the Marketing Plan contains details on the Marketing Mix Elements (product strategy, pricing strategy, channel of distribution strategy, marketing communications strategy).

It is for this reason that some businesses do not develop a separate Strategic Plan and a separate Marketing Plan. Instead, they combine the two plans into one document called the Strategic Marketing Plan.

As can be seen from Exhibit 3.1, the Marketing Plan is a crucial document to develop because it spawns other functional plans such as Sales Plans, Manufacturing Plans, HR Plans, IT Plans, etc. In other words, the Marketing Plan, with its analysis of markets, customers, segments, competitors, provides a common foundation (context) for the development of other functional plans (please see Chapter 7 for details on an annual planning calendar to link different plans).

However, notice the two-way arrows in the Exhibit. Clearly, while the Marketing Plan sets the context for the development of other Functional Plans, it is also influenced by them (details on this are found in Chapter 7).

Collectively, these functional plans in many organizations are called the Annual Operating Plan

The crucial direction given by the Marketing Plan is necessary for other functions to develop their own plans. It is in this way that the business achieves enterprise alignment – each function is squarely concerned with implementing the overall strategic direction of the business. All functions are thus tied together with a common thread – understanding customers, creating value for them, delivering the value and managing the value created.

Based on the commitments made in the functional plans, the business allocates resources for the coming year (capital allocation and budgets). A set of key performance metrics (KPMs) is put in place to measure actual performance against targets. Any variance is analyzed and this closes the planning loop. Essentially, the business learns from the implementation of its strategy and uses this knowledge to update the Strategic Plan for the next 3 – 5 year horizon.

The Marketing Plan, while containing details on markets and customers, is also not a very implementable document – it does not offer any guidance to a sales professional seated in front of a customer.

In other words, the Marketing Plan should be *translated* into Sales and Key Account (Customer) Plans because it is these plans that get implemented because they contain details on how each customer will be treated. (In Chapter 6 I provide details on how to make the connection between the Marketing Plan and Sales and Customer Plans.)

Why Develop A Marketing Plan?

Think of a Marketing Plan as a roadmap for your business. In everyday life, we develop plans, or roadmaps, to help guide our efforts. For example, when we go on a picnic we have to plan to ensure the picnic is successful. We ask such questions as:

- Where do we want to go for a picnic?
- Who is going to make travel arrangements?
- What food are we going to eat?
- Who will bring what type of food?
- How are we going to keep the ants away? (Answer: Give them a picnic of their own!)
- What fun activities are we going to do?
- What will we do in case it rains?
- How much is it going to cost us?

Without a plan, or roadmap, you could end up with a lot of potato salad on your picnic and no hamburgers. Or, you may find after you get there that the park you wanted to go to was closed. Or, it may rain and ruin your beautiful outing.

Why should your business be any different? Why would you want to compete in a cutthroat environment without any formal plan?   While this may seem obvious to you, you may be surprised to learn just how many businesses simply drift along for years without any formal strategic planning.

The sad reality is that, eventually, these businesses fail and end up being another statistic in the Business Hall of Shame.

A Marketing Plan enables you to improve the odds for success

A Marketing Plan enables you to improve your odds for success by:

- Disciplining you to think about your customers and their needs, both today and in the future.
- Anticipating what competitors are lurking in the bushes, waiting to take customers away from you and ambush your business.
- Asking you to think about how attractive the market for your good or service is, and what slice of the pie you can get.
- Thinking about strategies and tactics to employ for your business to succeed in the marketplace.
- Contingency plans in case things do not work out the way you anticipated.
- Continually revisiting your strategies and tactics to ensure that your thinking is correct, thereby enabling your business to evolve over time and adapt to the needs of an ever-changing marketplace.
- Developing a Marketing Plan enables you to integrate all of your company's activities. It provides everyone with a common focus.
- Focusing your efforts and utilizing precious resources strategically for maximum impact. Without a Marketing Plan a business tends to diffuse its efforts, acting constantly in a tactical fashion, without any strategic thinking.

"Measure Twice, Cut Once"
...Old Chinese Saying

Actually, when I was in China helping a business develop Marketing Plans the Chinese told me that the real proverb says "Measure thrice (not twice) and cut once!" The ancients sure knew what they were talking about and we can learn a lot about running a business from them.

As I said earlier, success in the business world depends upon careful planning and execution of strategies. The number one reason why businesses fail is because they fail to plan. This chapter ends with a template you can use to develop superior Marketing Plans for your business.

However, before you examine the Marketing Plan Template, take a look at Exhibit 3.2. In it, I provide some valuable notes you should read before you start working with the Template.

EXHIBIT 3.2   Notes to Accompany Marketing Plan Template

> ➢ A good Marketing Plan should be a highly *actionable* document that everyone within the team should follow.
> ➢ The Marketing Plan should guide and focus your daily activities.
> ➢ Keep the Plan to around 20 pages or 40 PowerPoint slides.
> ➢ As necessary, individual plans may be developed for each product line or product (services offered, programs, brands, etc.).
> ➢ The Marketing Plan should be developed for a period of one year. However, it is necessary to meet periodically (e.g., every quarter) to assess progress and make any corrections to the Plan. You will find more details on this topic in Chapter 7.
> ➢ The Marketing Plan template should not be viewed as a checklist; rather, examine the *essence* of each section to assess what it is asking of you.

Strategic Marketing Plan Template[10]

Section 1. Executive Summary
- Key challenges facing my business
- Key strategies to be implemented during the next year
- Key anticipated outcomes for the business

---

[10] The next chapter contains detailed notes on using this template. Remember, this is a generic Marketing Plan template and may need to be adapted to suit your needs. The template is equally applicable – whether you are developing a plan in business-to-business markets or business-to-consumer markets. Appendix 1 contains an example of a superior Marketing Plan.

Section 2. Table of Contents

Section 3. Marketplace Analysis
How attractive is the market: Analysis by segments we compete in
- Description of market segments we currently serve (or want to serve, for a new business)
- Forecast of market potential and rate of growth
- Market share of key players
- Historic sales volume, revenue, profit, share by target segment
- Market assumptions driving current Marketing Plan

Distribution trends
- Major channel members and balance of power
- Major trends in distribution that could impact our business
- Any other trends (such as decline of one channel member or emergence of new channel) that could impact our business

Pricing trends
- What are some trends in pricing that could impact our business
- Analysis by market segments, customers, products (goods and services), and channels of distribution

Analysis of the macroenvironment that could affect our business
- Demographic factors
- Socio/cultural factors
- Economic factors
- Technological factors
- Political/regulatory factors

Summary of major implications of marketplace analysis
- For business development, new product development, sales strategies, service strategies, operational excellence, marketing communication tools, etc.

Section 4. Competitive Analysis
Format: In main body of Marketing Plan 1 or 2 pages of competitive analysis summary, indicating what *we* need to do to become a more competitive player in each market segment. In Appendix, 1 page profiling each major competitor on factors listed as follows.

<u>In Appendix, for each competitor in market segments we serve (current and new competitors planning entry into market)</u>
- Size
- Goals
- Market share
- Product mix (products offered)
- Product quality/capability
- Strengths
- Weaknesses
- Opportunities
- Threats
- How they currently serve *our* customer segments
- Likely future moves
- Other pertinent information that highlights their intentions in this market
- Leverage points they can use against us
- Our competitive advantage over them
- *Implications for how we can more effectively compete against this competitor*

<u>Competitive summary (in main body of Marketing Plan)</u>
- Implications for us in terms of how we can compete more effectively: new product development, sales strategies, service, business development, etc.

Section 5. Segmentation Analysis: Markets and Customers
- Segmentation analysis (in main body of Marketing Plan provide summary; in appendix provide details on each segment)
    - Market segments we compete in: Analysis of needs and trends
    - Market segment attractiveness: Based on segment growth, penetration and profitability
    - New market segments: needs and trends
- Customer Analysis
    - Customer segments we serve
    - Customer needs – current and future. (Use value chain analysis to go beyond the obvious.[11])
    - Key decision making criteria used by customers
    - Key decision making personnel and their needs
    - Customer satisfaction levels
    - Customer segment attractiveness: Based on growth, penetration and profitability
- Develop market x customer grid to identify need profiles (as shown in Chapter 2)

---

[11] Details provided in next chapter.

Major implications of segmentation analysis
- Segments (markets and customers) we should focus on, implications for new product development, sales strategies, service, business development, pricing, marketing communications, etc.

Section 6. Assessment of Opportunities, Threats, Strengths, Weaknesses and Key Issues
Format: One page of bulleted key opportunities and key threats for side-by-side comparison. One page of bulleted key strengths and key weaknesses for side-by-side comparison.
- Opportunities/threats analysis
- Strengths/weaknesses of organization (to respond to opportunities and threats) analysis
- Analysis of past marketing effort
  - What we did right last year
  - What we did wrong
  - What lessons we learned
  - Analysis of last year's marketing strategy: What gaps exist in our strategy and implementation?
  - Which strategies from last year should we keep?[12]
  - Market segment review: trends and profitability
  - Customer mix review by segment: trends and profitability
  - Product mix review by segment: trends and profitability
  - Segmentation review: does our segmentation scheme provide us with a competitive advantage in the marketplace? If not, can we think of alternate segmentation methods?
  - What business are we in? How does this impact what markets we serve and how?
- Business implications of data collected about marketplace and our business
  - What does this information mean for us?
  - What are some major business implications in terms of how we should serve customers and compete in each segment?
- Issues analysis
  - Key issues to be addressed by the business based on above analyses
    - Next year
    - Years 1 – 5 (prioritize, if necessary, by year)

---

[12] This year's strategy should be a continuation of last year. Flip flopping on strategy is a certain road to eventual failure.

Section 7. Objectives By Segment

- Overall direction for each segment
- Marketing objectives
  - Market share
  - Market development
  - Market penetration
  - New product objectives
  - Product modification objectives
  - Customer service objectives
  - Sales objectives
  - Channel of distribution objectives
  - Marketing communication objectives
  - Pricing objectives
- Financial objectives
  - Sales volume
  - Revenue
  - Profitability
- Other objectives

Section 8. Marketing Strategies by Segment[13]

Product/offering strategy

- Product/offering benefits and customer value created (be explicit in terms of increasing customer revenues or decreasing customer cost)
- Service strategy
- Expected product modifications/improvements; implications for new product development

Channel of distribution strategy

- Is true potential of a channel being realized?
- Channel design issues
- How do we plan to serve end customers by creating value for channel members?

---

[13] Ensure selected strategies are in line with Key Issues identified in Section 6. For example, Section 6 may identify being a systems (total solutions) provider as a way to compete. Our strategies should reflect this.

Ensure selected strategies are in line with overall corporate strategy.

Marketing communications strategy
- Who do we want to communicate to?
- What strategic objectives do we want to achieve via our communication efforts? What is the message we are trying to communicate to the target market?
- How should we communicate (tactical execution details)?
- How will we measure our communication effectiveness?

Pricing strategy
- By product, service, segment, channel
- Are pricing strategies in line with proposed value creation efforts under product/offering strategies?

Supply chain strategy

Other strategies needed to make Marketing Plan a success
- Sales strategy
- Marketing research strategies
- Operations
- Human resources
- Other strategies
- Cross-functional implications of Marketing strategies[14]

Section 9. Marketing Plan Implementation (Tactics)
Specifically, for *each* strategy item identified in the previous section delineate:
- What will be done (tactics)?
- When will it be done (timeline)
- Who will do it (e.g., functional department or interaction between departments)?
- What help will be needed (resources)?
- Contingency plans in event of blockage of Marketing Plan execution?

Section 10. Positioning Relative to Competition
- In this section examine how your strategies and tactics will give your business a competitive advantage over your competitors.
- Also, outline how this year's Plan is superior to the one developed last year.

---

[14] By outlining cross-functional implications of Marketing strategy, we ensure that the Marketing Plan indeed unifies the corporation by highlighting how different functions need to work together to optimize the health of the enterprise. Appendix 1 (Marketing Plan example) contains details on this.

Section 11. Marketing – Sales Linkage
- Use the segment x customer grid developed during needs analysis to identify segment value propositions. This matrix forms the foundation for development of Sales and Key Account (Customer) Plans.
- Special needs of key customers
- Identify and prioritize target customers within each market segment
- Identify key prospects within each market segment
- Identify how the Marketing – Sales linkage will take place within your organization.

Section 12. Key Outcomes for the Business
- Revenue and profit impact of strategies
- Sales volumes
- Market share
- Revenue
- Profitability
- Return on investment (ROI)

Section 13. Marketing Plan Budget

Section 14. Marketing Plan Control
Delineate how the execution of the Marketing Plan will be monitored
For key Marketing and Financial objectives, identify:
- Goals to be achieved by period
- Information needed to track above
    - What metrics will be secured?
    - Who will get the information?
    - Who will track progress toward goals by period?
    - When will team meet to review metrics to determine if Marketing Plan is on target?
- What mechanisms will be in place for testing Marketing Plan assumptions, taking corrective actions, etc.

Section 15. Appendix

Chapter 4

Marketing Plans: An Owner's Manual for the Template

In This Chapter You Will Find...

- An exercise in high school Chemistry: Distilling the Marketing Plan to its barest elements
- An easy-to-use "owner's manual" to develop strategic Marketing Plans
    - Executive summary
        - What should a good executive summary contain?
    - Table of contents
    - Marketplace analysis
        - Why is this market attractive and what are the major trends?
- Competitive analysis
        - What are competitors doing to take business away from us?
        - What should we be doing to become a better competitor?
    - Segmentation analysis: Markets and customers
        - Customer needs and value drivers by segment
        - Understanding customer needs: Value Chain Analysis
    - SWOT analysis
        - Opportunities and threats, followed by strengths and weaknesses
    - Identification of key issues facing your business
        - Focus of the Marketing Plan for the upcoming year
    - Setting segment objectives
        - What do we want to achieve?
    - Marketing strategies and tactics
        - How are we going to achieve our goals?
        - Cross-functional implications of Marketing strategy
    - Positioning relative to the competition
        - How will our strategies give us an advantage over our competitors?
    - Marketing – Sales linkage
        - How will the Sales – Marketing gap be bridged?
    - Key business outcomes
        - What rewards will we earn because of our hard work?
    - Marketing Plan budget
        - How much will our strategies cost us?
    - Marketing Plan control
        - How will we control Plan implementation and handle any changes?
    - Appendix
        - All support material goes in here

An Exercise In High School Chemistry

The Marketing Plan template outlined in the previous chapter has 14 sections to it (excluding the appendix). So, it may appear to you to be very complicated. Actually, the Marketing Plan is a very simple document.

Before reading further, I want you to try the exercise below.

Do you recall your high school Chemistry labs? I do. I had one particularly favorite exercise – distillation. In distillation, a fluid is heated in a bulbous container and the vapors pass through a squiggly tube where they condense. The tube ends in a small container where precious drops of liquid accumulate.

I want you to perform the same distillation task to our Marketing Plan template. Strip it of its details and see what remains (the distillate, so to speak). See if you can identify the main components of our Marketing Plan template.

Although it may look complicated, the Marketing Plan actually is a very simple document that has four *major* sections as outlined in Exhibit 4.1

EXHIBIT 4.1 Marketing Plan Sections

Sections 3, 4, 5
- Marketplace and competitive analysis
- Segmentation analysis: markets and customers

Sections 6, 7, 8
- Assessment of key issues facing the business
- Objectives and marketing strategies by segment

Sections 9, 10, 11
- Marketing Plan implementation
- Positioning relative to competition
- Marketing - Sales linkage

Sections 12, 13, 14
- Key outcomes for the business
- Marketing Plan budget and control

Does this four-section framework look familiar? It should, because in Chapter 2, we said that winning businesses succeed by understanding-creating-delivering-managing customer value, and the Marketing Plan is nothing but an embodiment of this framework.

As you can see, the four major sections of the Marketing Plan are there for a reason and they each play an important role in that the *output* from one section forms the *input* for the next section, and so on.

More Details On Each Section

Now that we have examined the Marketing Plan's overall structure, let us take a look at each of the 15 sections to see why they are there and what role they play in the overall Marketing Plan development.

> **But first, one word of advice: Do not treat the Plan template as a checklist. Instead, view the template as directional. That means, examine each section to ascertain what it is asking of you and proceed accordingly.**

Also, do not be concerned if you do not have data. For example, your understanding of customer needs may not be as detailed as you would like. Instead of letting this upset you, treat it as an opportunity. I am impressed when a manager tells me the following:

- "I know I do not have this data"
- "I know why it is important to have this data"
- "I know how to proceed to obtain this data"

Section 1. Executive Summary
The Executive Summary section is a summary of the Marketing Plan. A good Executive Summary should have these sections:

1. Key challenges facing my business
2. Key strategies to be implemented next year
3. Key anticipated outcomes for the business

Therefore, reading the Executive Summary tells us at a glance what strategies will be pursued to address key challenge facing the business and what rewards await us at the end of the Plan period if we implement our strategies well.

Keep the Executive Summary to 1 or 2 pages (or slides), not more. The Executive Summary is written for a busy executive who, after reading 1 or 2 pages, should be able to tell whether or not you have a good grasp of the challenges facing your business and what you plan to do about them. And, if the executive so wishes, there is always the main body of the Plan for more details.

I know managers who can develop 100-page Marketing Plans, but cannot tell you the top 3 issues facing their business. A good Executive Summary can tell a lot about your grasp of the main challenges facing your business.

The Executive Summary should be written last, after the Marketing Plan has been developed.

Section 2. Table of Contents
After the Executive Summary section a Table of Contents section appears so one can see what areas the Plan covers. This helps the reader navigate more easily through the Plan.

Even though this seems obvious, always provide page numbers in your Marketing Plan and a Table of Contents.

You will not believe the number of times I am asked to review a Plan without page numbers or a Table of Contents. This used to puzzle me until I asked a manager why his plan did not contain page numbers. This is what he said, "If you do not put page numbers or a table of contents you can insert or delete pages at the very last minute and not have to worry about redoing the table of contents section."

Of course, if this is how you run your business (just-in-time-panic-driven-effort) I suppose providing page numbers is a trivial matter.

Section 3. Marketplace Analysis

In this section we start by providing a description of the marketplace (segments) we serve. If you are a new business you would provide a description of segments you *want* to serve.

Then, we discuss how attractive the market is in terms of market potential (how big is this market), rate of growth, share of key players (including our share), and historic sales, revenues, share and profit trends.

Finally, we state the assumptions driving Marketing Plan development.

Essentially, this section is asking us to describe how attractive the markets we serve (or want to serve, for a new business) are.

Next, we examine the major distribution trends in each market. Distribution trends refer to evolving dynamics within the channel of distribution through which we operate. For example, an accurate reading of distribution trends would alert us to the decreasing importance of one channel member and the emergence of other channels such as Home Centers, or the changing role of wholesalers, or the importance of the internet in purchasing decisions. This enables us to be proactive in our design of channels of distribution strategies so we are always satisfying the needs of our customers.

Understanding distribution trends is key because, even if your business is doing very well, it could be heading for a disaster because your key customers (for example, wholesalers) could be going out of business or consolidating.

Similarly, understanding pricing trends in the marketplace enable us to be proactive in using this important, but often underutilized, marketing mix element in our marketing strategies. Our analysis may reveal, for example, that customers are moving away from short term pricing to more long term pricing arrangements with a reduced set of key suppliers. This information has crucial implications for what strategies we may pursue to satisfy and build relationships with our customers.

This section ends with a discussion about the major macro-environmental forces that could impact our business. These forces are demographic, socio-cultural, economic, technological or political. For example, we may, through our analysis, come to the conclusion that politicians are talking about introducing rent controls in the near future. This could have significant impact on how we compete because it may limit our business in terms of rents charged, which in turn, limits capital work that can be done to rental buildings.

Before you leave this section spend some time reflecting upon what you have learned about the marketplace (in other words, do not wait until you have collected data from all sections before starting to think about implications for running your business). What do the data mean for business development opportunities, sales strategies, etc.?

Section 4. Competitive Analysis

We do not operate in our markets in a vacuum. Our competitors are also trying to serve the needs of our customers through their *own* value-creation efforts. Therefore, in this section we examine the landscape to assess the opportunities, threats, strengths and weaknesses facing our current and potential competitors. Most importantly, we are keeping an eye on how they serve the needs of market segments we operate in. Therefore, the goal of this section is to provide us with an indication of how well our competitors are doing and an early warning of actions we might need to take in our unceasing efforts at serving customers.

Essentially, in the Competitive Analysis section we are asking the question, "What are our competitors doing to take business away from us and what should we be doing to become a more formidable competitor?"

My suggestion is to summarize your competitive analysis in the main body of the Marketing Plan by answering the above question. Put individual competitor profiles in the appendix of the Marketing Plan. Do not make the mistake I see in many Marketing Plans I review – detailed SWOT analyses on competitors without answering the basic question "What should we be doing to become a better competitor?"

> **Remember, you should constantly be asking the question: "What do the data mean in terms of how I should be running my business?"**

Section 5. Segmentation Analysis: Markets and Customers

The ultimate focus of our value creation efforts is the *customer*. If we are not creating and delivering superior strategies for the customer all of our efforts are for nothing. Therefore, in this section we examine customer needs and value drivers by segment and how these may be changing over time.

I am often asked about what determines the long-term success of any business. I think it is this:

> **The only sustainable competitive advantage an organization has is its ability to understand the needs of its customers faster and in a superior fashion to its competitors.**

What I mean is, without an accurate understanding of customer needs the business has no chance of ever satisfying needs. Later in this chapter we will see that it may not be enough to merely understand needs, but also to *create* them.

We start by examining the needs and trends of the segments we currently compete in (for example, from Exhibit 2.3, Pharmaceuticals, Manufacturing, Food). Then, we analyze the attractiveness of each segment based on:

A market segment's attractiveness is based on such factors as...

➢ Segment growth
➢ Segment penetration opportunities
➢ Segment profitability
➢ Strategic fit with our business

As shown in Exhibit 2.3 (and discussed in detail in Chapter 2), segmentation refers to the process of segmenting both *markets* and *customers* we serve.

So, we next turn to analyzing the needs of our customers.

We start by identifying the current customer segments we serve (for example, Premium, Performance, Value) and their needs. The most difficult part is identifying a customer's needs. We cannot simply ask our customers what their needs are because (a) they do not know or, (b) even if they do know they will state their needs in terms of what my friend Ron Spradley calls "Basic Care" variables. Let me give you a couple of examples.

Example 1

The hotel chain I normally stay at during my business travel to the West Coast asked me to fill out a customer satisfaction survey. I readily complied. The last question on the survey went something like this, "What other needs do you have that are not currently being satisfied?"

I was at a loss. I did not know how to answer this question. I wrote, "I have no unsatisfied needs that I can think of. I am a very satisfied customer."

The hotel manager, upon receipt of my survey would be overjoyed. She would assemble her staff and congratulate them. "See," she would say, "We received a perfect score, we will keep this customer for a long time."

And yet, I would be a prime candidate to switch brands if another hotel chain came along and, by an accurate understanding of my needs, *created* value for me by, say, putting a treadmill in my room upon request (which hotels do now), or by putting a personal chef at my disposal for the duration of my stay (which also hotels do now because they know that business travelers tend to abuse their bodies with improper nutrition).

The hotel manager would be left holding a perfect satisfaction score in her hand and wonder why the customer switched.

The sooner you understand this the more successful you will be:

1. **Your customers do not know what their needs are.**
2. **It is not their job to tell you what their needs are, it is *your* job to find out.**

Example 2

At the Schulich School of Business, where I teach, we have our MBA students do a final project where a group of students acts as a consultant to a business. A group of three faculty members advises each student group. The deliverable for the students is a strategy study for the client. The project lasts around six months.

I was an advisor to a student group whose client was a chain of mall-based stores selling vitamins and other supplements (I am sure you have seen the type) called the Nutrition Nook (I have disguised the name). The advisors were meeting with the students so the students could showcase three months of marketing research efforts to understand consumer needs.

This is what the students found. Consumers said they wanted these attributes in a Nutrition Nook store:

- Convenient location
- Good price points
- Good customer service
- Convenient hours
- Variety of merchandize
- Knowledgeable sales staff

What do you think of the above list? If you answered, "It is too generic. It could apply to any business on the face of this planet," you would be right.

What happened here? Were the students lazy? Absolutely not, they had worked very hard, indeed.

What happened is this – the students fell into a classic marketing research trap. And, it is this:

Ask an obvious question of your customer and you deserve an obvious answer.

What the students got is called "Basic Care". I would hope the Nutrition Nook has these basic attributes. But, they by themselves are not enough to give this business a competitive edge in the marketplace.

Example 3

Now for a business-to-business example. What would happen if you asked your customer the same question, "Tell me what your needs are?" This is what your customer would probably say:

- I need you to supply the product as specified
- I need you to deliver on time
- I need customer service support
- I need accurate invoicing
- And, did I mention I want a low price?

So you see, customers either do not know what their needs are or they will answer in terms of "Basic Care" issues. So, what I tell business leaders is:

Never ask customers, tell them.

I am not trying to be cute here, I will show you how. Use a technique called Value Chain Analysis to understand customer needs. An example of Value Chain Analysis is shown in Exhibit 4.2.

EXHIBIT 4.2   Value Chain Analysis

Lumber Supplier

⇩

- By understanding that the Sawmill (immediate customer) is part of a Value Chain, Lumber Supplier can create value propositions for Sawmill without ever having to ask, "What are your needs?"

Sawmill

⇩

- To create value for the Roof Truss Manufacturer, the Sawmill looks to the Lumber Supplier and asks, "What value can you create for me?"

Roof Truss Manufacturer

⇩

- To enable cutting Home Builder's repetitive cost of labor by 10%, Roof Truss Manufacturer turns to his supplier (Sawmill) for help.

Home Builder

⇩

- Home Builder wants to satisfy SOHO Customer needs, but does not know how because building an office will increase cost of home.
- Home Builder cannot pass on increased cost to Home Buyer because customer will not pay more.
- So, Home Builder asks his supplier (Roof Truss Manufacturer) to cut his repetitive cost of labor by 10%.

Home Buyer (SOHO Customer)

- Small Office Home Office (SOHO) Customer operates business from home. So, wants Home Builder to build an office in her home.
- But, SOHO Customer does not want the office to be located at the back of the house, wants the office to be built by the front door.
- Does not want to pay Home Builder more money for the house.

Let us examine the Value Chain from the Lumber Supplier's perspective. The Sawmill is the Lumber Supplier's customer. However, what happens when the Lumber Supplier asks the Sawmill, "What are your needs?" The Sawmill owner is likely to reply, "My needs are to receive the product according to my specifications, delivered on time, invoiced accurately, with customer service support. Oh, did I mention I want a low price?"

As we can see asking the customer about their needs only reveals Basic Care variables. To understand customer needs and create value for the Sawmill the Lumber Supplier has to recognize that the Sawmill is part of a chain of suppliers and customers creating value for each other.

To use the power of the value chain, the Lumber Supplier should start at the bottom of the chain and examine trends among Home Buyers. What the Lumber Supplier might discover is this – an emergence of a customer called the SOHO (Small Office Home Office) customer.

The SOHO customer is an entrepreneur who runs her business from her home. Because of this, she needs an office in her home. What she tells the Home Builder is this. "I will buy a home from you if you can put an office in my home. But, I know what will happen if I leave you to your own devices. You will locate the office at the back of the house (because this is more cost-effective for you).

This is not good for me because when my customers visit my office they have to go through my kitchen and see my dirty dishes in my sink before they get to my office. I don't like this because I want to project a professional appearance. For this reason I want you to put the office by the front door. If you can do this you have my business. Otherwise, I'm going to go and look down the street. Oh, and did I forget to mention that I'm not going to pay you any more for the house?"

The Home Builder wants to sell a home to the SOHO customer, but is faced with higher costs because of the SOHO customer's unique requirements. So, who do you think the Home Builder turns to? The Roof Truss Manufacturer, of course. The Homer Builder tells the Roof Truss Manufacturer, "I will give you my business if you can reduce my repetitive cost of labor by 10%. Currently, I have to do some assembly work on-site after you deliver the goods."

Who do you think the Roof Truss Manufacturer turns to? His supplier , the Sawmill, of course. And so it goes up the value chain. Therefore, if the Lumber Supplier wants to understand the needs of his customer he has to understand how his customer (Sawmill) creates value for his customer (Roof Truss Manufacturer). By understanding the dynamics of the value chain the Lumber Supplier can go to his customer and tell him the value he can create for him, without asking the Sawmill, "Tell me what your needs are?"

There are other items we need to include in the Segmentation Analysis: Markets and Customers section. We need to understand how our customers make decisions. To understand this we need to understand criteria used by our customers to make decisions and how those criteria are applied. Let me share with you two examples.

A tour operator trying to sell vacation packages needs to understand what criteria a family might use to choose between different vacation destinations and vacation types. Also, the tour operator would need to know what roles different family members play and what criteria each of them have. So, the children may influence the decision, but the parents actually make the decision (based on a different set of criteria).

A business organization is no different from the family making a decision. The difference is that in business organizations the decision criteria and decision making process is typically more formal.

We also need to understand customer satisfaction levels with the usage of our goods and services. Of course, if you are a new business this will apply only once you have been in business for a while. Satisfaction levels are important to measure because they enable us to make *process improvements* such as how our goods and services are delivered to customers. But, customer satisfaction measurement is a poor way to *understand* customer needs.

Just as we did with market segments, we need to understand how attractive our customer segments are using similar criteria as before:

> A customer segment's attractiveness is based on such factors as…
>
> ➢ Customer segment growth
> ➢ Customer segment penetration opportunities
> ➢ Customer segment profitability
> ➢ Customer segment strategic fit

Just I showed in Exhibit 2.3, I strongly recommend that the end result of this analysis should reveal a market x customer grid, with each cell in the grid containing your analysis of needs.

Finally, end this section by reflecting upon the implications of what you have learned for how you should be running your business. This could include such issues as segments you should be focusing on, segments you should be getting out of, new product development implications, etc.

> **Therefore, at the end of Section 5 we have completed a scan of the major forces in the marketplace. We are now ready to synthesize this information to see what it means to us (in our capabilities to create value for our customers).**

Section 6. Assessment of Opportunities, Threats, Strengths, Weaknesses and Key Issues

Collecting information about the marketplace in sections 3, 4, and 5 will not help us very much unless we reduce this information so we can answer one basic question: *What does this all mean for us in terms of how we should be competing in the marketplace?*

Therefore, in this section we first examine the major opportunities and threats facing us in the marketplace based on our assessment in the previous sections. Then, we analyze our ability to respond to these opportunities and threats. We do this by examining our strengths and weaknesses. So, what we have just conducted is a SWOT analysis (strengths, weaknesses, opportunities and threats analysis).

Did you notice that I am asking you to examine opportunities and threats first, and *then* strengths and weaknesses? Typically, you may have been taught to examine strengths and weaknesses first, and *then* opportunities and threats. So, what I am recommending is that you conduct an OTSW analysis, instead of a SWOT analysis.

You should follow my recommendations for these reasons:

- Examining strengths and weaknesses *before* opportunities and threats simply does not make any sense. I see this mistake being made all the time. A manager will list the business' strengths and weaknesses *independent* of their impact on opportunities and threats. For example, the manager will write in the Marketing Plan, "A key strength is our strong relationship with wholesalers." However, later in the Marketing Plan one reads that wholesalers are going out of business, and being replaced by, say, home garden centers. In other words, strong relationships with wholesales is not a strength. In fact, this business is headed for deep trouble because they do not have any relationships built with home garden centers.
- In other words, a strength is not a strength unless it enables you to capitalize on an opportunity or enables you to mitigate a threat.
- Similarly, a weakness is not a weakness unless it impacts your ability to capture an opportunity or minimize a threat.
- Examining opportunities and threats *first* enables you to consider what is possible for your business without the imposition of constraints. It enables you to think big, pay attention to the marketplace, instead of starting with an internal (myopic) focus.
- Therefore, you should first examine what the external environment is telling you in terms of how you should compete in the marketplace. Then, you should examine your capabilities to do so.
- The sequence I have recommended (OTSW instead of SWOT) will enable you to consider resource requirements to take advantage of external opportunities or to mitigate threats.

Remember…

Opportunities and Threats are external.

Strengths and Weaknesses are internal.

Of course, I clearly understand why you have been taught to do a SWOT analysis – one can actually pronounce it. OTSW is impossible to pronounce!

I would rather you have difficulties with pronunciation than difficulties competing in the marketplace.

Next, analyze your past Marketing efforts: What did you do right last year? What lessons has your business learned?   What gaps exist in your strategy and implementation?

Conduct a thorough review of your products and customers by segment. Which ones are profitable?   Which ones are not?   In other words, every business should periodically examine:

- Which segments it competes in
- Which segments it should be entering and exiting
- Which customers it serves
- Which customers it should be developing and dropping
- With what goods and services it satisfies market needs (that is, the product mix)
- What goods and services should be added (new product development), and what goods and services should be deleted

Which customers are taking up too much of your resources without giving anything in return?

When we discussed segmentation in Chapter 2 perhaps you came to one inescapable conclusion:

The process of market segmentation should give your business a competitive advantage in the market. If it does not, you have a me-too segmentation scheme.

So, in this section examine your segmentation scheme and see if you can segment your markets in a different way. For example, the building products business we have discussed previously used to segment its markets by domestic customers and export customers. They recognized that this was not giving them a competitive advantage in the marketplace (because the unimaginative segmentation scheme was not enabling them to satisfy hidden needs or segments).

By segmenting their markets by Repair and Remodeling customers, Home Builders and Industrial Customers, they uncovered innovative ways in which they could satisfy customer needs. For example, they developed a line of pre-fabricated products (floors, walls) to reduce home builders' on-site labor costs.

They trained the sales force at big box retailers to help Do-It-Yourself customers (also called Over-the-Shoulder business – customers who do repair and remodeling tasks on their homes on their own, without the help of a contractor) make more informed decisions about plywood purchases.

Your segmentation analysis will be greatly enhanced if you ponder a more global question – What business are we in?

This type of thinking is crucial for any business to undertake. Without it, the tendency is to focus on what we do and not on the impact on the customer.

The building products company used to believe they were in the lumber business (a classic mistake made by many organizations who focus on their core goods or services). Upon further reflection they came to the conclusion that their real business was not lumber, but building products. This enabled them to re-segment their markets and offer the innovations previously discussed.

Before you write down the main issues to be addressed by the Marketing Plan, go away and spend some time thinking about the information you have learned about the marketplace and your business (customers, competitors, markets, major opportunities and threats, strengths and weaknesses). Ask some fundamental questions such as: What does this mean for us? So what? What are the implications of the information we have just gathered? Does this mean we have to …?

Now write your thoughts down in the form of main issues that will need to be addressed by the Marketing Plan. Prioritize the issues you need to tackle, recognizing that you will not be able to do everything next year. This is how your

Marketing Plan truly becomes a document for developing superior business strategies.

For example, let us say that your SWOT analysis reveals a major opportunity for your business – mid-size customers are a very attractive segment and are currently not being served by competitors. However, examination of your weaknesses reveals that you do not have any capability to serve this customer segment.

So, a key issue to be addressed by the Marketing Plan next year is to develop capabilities (goods, services, channels of distribution, etc.) to serve this customer segment. [15]

As you can see, up to this point we have taken a survey of the marketplace and we have come to certain conclusions about what major issues we will have to address during the next year. Now it should be fairly clear to you what actions you will need to take next year to serve the market well and be an effective competitor.

At this point the Marketing Plan should *almost* write itself (with your help!).

Section 7. Objectives By Segment

In the previous section we identified the major issues to be addressed by the Marketing Plan. While these issues tell us what we need to tackle (for example, developing a product aimed at the mid-market customer), they do not provide specific guidelines. It is for this reason we develop objectives we want to achieve by segment.

We begin by outlining the overall direction we want to take for each segment. So, we may decide that the Health and Beauty segment is very attractive and we want to achieve a greater level of penetration in this segment.

---

[15]   In the Marketing Plan example in Appendix 1 you will see more examples of how the business has identified key issues to be addressed by conducting a SWOT analysis.

More specifically, we set some Marketing objectives in such terms as share, new product, etc. We also state Sales objectives for the segment (although at this point the Sales objectives may not be as specific as we would like it to be; as you will see, when we develop Sales and Customer Plans we outline very specific objectives).

We also set Financial objectives for each segment in such terms as revenue and profitability.

Other objectives (for example, Human Resource) may also be set.

> **Marketing objectives enable us to develop specific marketing actions. We turn to this in the next section.**

Section 8. Marketing Strategies by Segment

This section is the engine that drives the Marketing Plan. It outlines our efforts to create value for customers using marketing mix elements and garner a competitive advantage for ourselves in the marketplace.

We begin by outlining strategies for the marketing mix elements: product/offering, channels of distribution, marketing communications, and price.

We also outline any other strategies (e.g., supply chain, production, etc.) we may have to implement in our value creation efforts. Therefore, in this section it is very useful if you examine the *cross-functional* implications of Marketing strategy – what each function needs to do to achieve business objectives identified in Section 7 (more details on this can be found in Chapter 7 and Appendix 1).

> **Strategies by themselves will not enable us to create value for our customers unless we implement them successfully. In the next section we outline implementation (tactical) plans.**

Section 9. Marketing Plan Implementation (Tactics)

In this section we examine our strategies in the previous section and for *each* strategy we delineate our tactical plans. We have to be very specific about what needs to be done (action steps), when it will be done, who will do it, what resources will be needed, and what we will do in case of a blockage of our Plan.

Many Marketing Plans go astray because they do not have this section. This is the way we assign responsibility for implementing the Plan. This is our way of ensuring that the Plan does not get written and put on a shelf somewhere to be forgotten.

The Tactics section ensures that the Marketing Plan guides our day-to-day efforts. Without this, our efforts tend to be rather diffuse, we do things that may be opportunistic, but not necessarily in the long term interests of the business.

Section 10. Positioning Relative to Competition

If we have formulated superior strategies, they should provide us with a superior position vis-à-vis the competition. Therefore, in this section state:

*   How your Marketing Plan will give you an edge in the marketplace
*   How this year's Plan is superior to the one you developed last year

Section 11. Marketing – Sales Linkage

I chose the title of this book *Marketing Led -- Sales Driven* on purpose. If you do not build a system for Marketing and Sales to work together, you are not harnessing the power and unique capabilities of each function.

It is for this reason that, in this section, you should do the following:

➢ Use the market segment x customer grid developed during customer needs analysis to identify segment value propositions (see the sample Marketing Plan included in this book). Without this crucial input the Sales function cannot develop meaningful Sales and Customer Plans.
➢ Identify and prioritize target customers and objectives by customer.
➢ Identify how the Marketing Plan will be translated into Sales and Customer Plans (more on this in Chapter 6).

Section 12. Key Outcomes for the Business

In this section we examine what rewards we hope to attain if we design and implement our strategies correctly. So we examine what share, volume and revenues our strategies will generate and what levels of profitability and Return on Investment (ROI) we can look forward to.

Section 13. Marketing Plan Budget

In this section outline the costs associated with the Marketing Plan. What have you budgeted for implementing strategies associated with the Marketing Plan?

Section 14. Marketing Plan Control

A Marketing Plan is a living, breathing document.

As such, it needs to be monitored constantly to ensure goals are being met and progress is being made. If not, corrective actions should be taken to bring the Plan back on track. Also, we need to assess whether the assumptions that went into Plan development are still valid.

Notice that in this section we assign responsibility for collecting information to assess whether the Plan is on track or not. Without this crucial section a Marketing Plan is just another document that gets written but is not acted upon.

Section 15. Appendix

Put all your supporting documentation in this section. The main body of the Marketing Plan should only contain the analysis, not the raw data. For example, examine in the main body of the Marketing Plan implications from the Competitive Analysis section in terms of how you can become a stronger competitor. But, do not put detailed information on each competitor in there, it belongs in the Appendix.

I am recommending this approach because:

➢ This will force you to be disciplined and think about the *implications* of your data. Otherwise, data collection tends to become an end in itself.
➢ The main body of your Marketing Plan will be crisp and hard-hitting.
➢ In my experience encyclopedic Plans do not get acted upon.

Chapter 5

Avoiding Common Pitfalls In Developing Marketing Plans

In This Chapter You Will Find...

➢ Tips on avoiding common pitfalls in developing superior Marketing Plans
  ➢ Focus on key strategies and tactics
  ➢ Understand the difference between a strategy and a tactic
  ➢ Distinguish between a key issue and a key fact
  ➢ Do not state the obvious in your Marketing Plan
  ➢ Do not benchmark against your competitors
  ➢ Keep the Plan short and simple
    ➢ Do not feed the data monster

  ➢ Do not forget that the Marketing Plan template is directional
  ➢ Spend a lot of time on Section 6 (assessment of opportunities, threats, strengths, weaknesses and key issues)
  ➢ Ensure your strategies match the data
  ➢ Ensure that your understanding of customer needs is not superficial
  ➢ Educate your organization on developing strategic Marketing Plans
  ➢ Remind people that Marketing is everyone's job
  ➢ Make Marketing Plan development part of a manager's scorecard
  ➢ Do not forget it takes courage to develop and implement superior Marketing Plans

A Marketing Plan should be an actionable document. It should guide your day-to-day business activities by the discipline it imposes on you to *focus* your efforts for maximum impact. A Marketing Plan is like a playbook for a team, without it the team flounders.

In other words, a Marketing Plan is not meant to be developed and put on someone's shelf to gather dust. Unfortunately, this is exactly what happens in many corporations.

In my experience, many times managers develop Marketing Plans because it is expected of them. However, the business is actually run without much relationship to the Marketing Plan.

I also find that superior plans are clearly customer focused, are proactive, and outline differentiated strategies to address the market. Managers who develop these plans exhibit an entrepreneurial spirit (as if they owned the business) and boldness of strategies. It is hard to explain, but I find superior plans have a sense of joy to them.

However, I find that average and inferior plans are about conducting business as usual, they lack focus, bring parity with the competition (at best), and exhibit a sense of defeatism.

Follow my recommendations below to ensure your team develops and implements a Plan with enthusiasm and success.

- **Focus on key strategies and tactics**

As we saw in Exhibit 3.1, the Marketing Plan is the foundation upon which all other operational plans are built. Therefore, the Marketing Plan is the bridge between the Strategic Plan for the business and the various functional plans. Keep the focus of the Marketing Plan on key strategies and tactics to be implemented for the period of one year.

Do not try to do it all in one year. Prioritize your options. Put down what you will accomplish next year and then also state what will be done in years 2, 3, etc. In this way, your Marketing Plan will become truly a strategic document.

- **Understand the difference between a strategy and a tactic**

A common mistake I find in business plans in general is the failure to distinguish between a strategy and a tactic. Consider these "strategy" statements (lifted from actual Marketing Plans):

-- We need to develop an electronic customer newsletter, or

-- We will attend more tradeshows next year.

These are tactics because, for an action to be called a strategy it should impact at least one of the following three questions; if it does not, it is a tactic.

A. Who do we serve (that is, what customers)?
B. How do we serve them (that is, with what goods and services)?
C. Who do we compete against?

So, while the decision to add a new line of baked goods to the product mix by a coffee house chain may be a tactic, the decision to sell pre-made coffee drinks in bottles through supermarkets by the same coffee chain would be considered a strategic move.

Finally, recognize that internal focus, business efficiency programs, and cost cutting measures are *not* strategies. I am amazed at how many CEOs, when asked about their plans for a business, cite business efficiency and cost cutting measures as "strategic moves".

•   Distinguish between a key issue and a key fact

Another common mistake I find in plans is the failure to distinguish between a key fact and a key issue. Recall from chapters 3 and 4 that the focus of Section 6 in the Marketing Plan template is to identify a set of *key issues* the business plans to address in the coming year. Not properly understanding the difference between the two leads to weak plan development.

Here is an example of a key fact: The industry faces declining shipments in flexo-widgets.

Now, here is the corresponding key issue: Declining industry shipments in flexo-widgets compel us to focus on value-added segments with margin opportunity.

Do you see the difference? A key fact is just that – a statement of what is. A key issue, on the other hand, is what *you* plan to do to *address* the key fact.

I recently read a Marketing Plan where the manager bemoaned the dismal state of his industry for nine pages, without once stating what he planned to do to address this key fact. I often tell managers that they are not being paid to make the obvious happen (or to state the obvious) – anyone can do that. What a senior executive wants to know is – in spite of the dismal state of the industry, what do *you* plan to do to compete and make the not-so-obvious happen?

•   Do not state the obvious in your Marketing Plan

Remember the following.

Your Marketing Plan should…

➢ Make you money.
➢ It should garner you a competitive edge in the marketplace. Many Marketing Plans I read enable the business to achieve par with their competition, *at best*. This is not acceptable. A Marketing Plan should provide your business with an edge in the marketplace. If your Marketing Plan is not doing this, I suggest you look at your understanding of customer needs. *A common reason for average Marketing Plans is a lack of in-depth understanding of customer needs.*
➢ A good Marketing Plan should be a page turner, it should tell a story. I am amazed at the mediocre Plans I am sent by clients to read and evaluate. I often wonder what these managers do at their desks all day. The Plans are based on superficial understanding of customer needs which in turn, lead to superficial strategies.

•   Do not benchmark against your competitors

Benchmarking against your competitors may sound appealing, but it is a slippery slope. Emulating your competitors will only get you to their level, *at best* (usually a smart competitor will have moved on to better things by the time you catch up).

I came across this statement in a Marketing Plan: "We should benchmark against Competitor X because they have the best service platform in the industry." I immediately contacted the business manager and expressed my concerns over such a move. We agreed to dig further and ask customers. What we found was very insightful.

Customers told us that they were willing to tradeoff inferior service if we could help them in other areas (e.g., product innovation or marketing research). Had we not asked our customers, the knee jerk reaction would have been to spend enormous sums of money to build up our service platform to match a competitor's. Instead, we found ways of competing effectively by focusing on our strengths.

Research shows that the model is compensatory, that is, your customers will most probably be willing to accept a lower standard on one dimension if you can help them with other pressing issues.

• Keep the Plan short and simple

Limit the Marketing Plan to around 20 pages or slides (if you prefer). To accomplish this, you will need to do these things:

> Do not feed the data monster. The data monster has an insatiable appetite for data. Subject your data to the litmus test and ask, "What does this data mean for how I should be competing in the marketplace?" If you cannot answer this question, the data do not belong in your Plan.

> Simplify tables and charts to their essentials. I have shown you an example in Exhibits 5.1 and 5.2 (like a "before" "after" portrait, if you wish). In Exhibit 5.1 (taken from an actual Marketing Plan, but with disguised data) the business manager has provided a lot of pricing data by quarter, but upon reading it I have little clue what it means. What this manager should have done is provide the graph shown in Exhibit 5.2, which essentially tells us that there is a downward pressure on pricing. What would *you* rather read – a whole bunch of numbers or a graph showing what the numbers mean?

> Put supporting material in the Appendix section. The main body of your Marketing Plan should only contain analyses.

> Do not wallow in your business' complexity, step back from it. I have shown you this in Exhibits 5.3 and 5.4. As you can see from Exhibit 5.4, the person writing this Plan is actually saying something very simple in a very complex fashion.

EXHIBIT 5.1   Pricing Trends

Price/Ton	Qtr 1 ($)			Qtr 2 ($)			Qtr 3 ($)			Qtr 4 ($)		
Widget A	1	2	Avg	1	2	Avg	1	2	Avg	1	2	Avg
Market 1	46.93	52.59	49.76	50.73	54.21	52.47	47.19	47.64	7.42	9.35	51.37	5.36
Market 2	49.92	50.15	50.04	49.94	56.59	53.26	48.13	50.70	49.41	36.86	53.88	45.37

Price/Ton	Qtr 1 ($)			Qtr 2 ($)			Qtr 3 ($)			Qtr 4 ($)		
Widget B	1	2	Avg	1	2	Avg	1	2	Avg	1	2	Avg
Market 1	37.97	36.34	37.15	36.50	37.82	37.16	40.22	35.33	37.77	30.21	40.10	35.16
Market 2	35.46	39.02	37.25	38.72	37.18	37.95	35.53	36.58	36.06	30.41	38.45	34.43

Price/Ton	Qtr 1 ($)			Qtr 2 ($)			Qtr 3 ($)			Qtr 4 ($)		
Nut A	1	2	Avg	1	2	Avg	1	2	Avg	1	2	Avg
Market 1	11.92	8.75	10.33	9.55	8.01	8.78	7.35	7.07	7.21	4.44	8.56	6.50
Market 2	9.19	10.30	9.74	10.09	9.93	10.01	7.92	8.71	8.31	5.36	9.57	7.46

Price/Ton	Qtr 1 ($)			Qtr 2 ($)			Qtr 3 ($)			Qtr 4 ($)		
Nut B	1	2	Avg	1	2	Avg	1	2	Avg	1	2	Avg
Market 1	4.33	4.34	4.33	3.94	4.04	3.99	4.29	3.47	3.88	2.77	5.15	3.96
Market 2	6.39	8.23	7.31	6.95	7.77	7.36	5.56	7.42	6.49	5.22	7.62	6.42

Price/Ton	Qtr 1 ($)			Qtr 2 ($)			Qtr 3 ($)			Qtr 4 ($)		
Bolt A	1	2	Avg	1	2	Avg	1	2	Avg	1	2	Avg
Market 1	4.33	4.34	4.33	3.94	4.04	3.99	4.29	3.47	3.88	2.77	5.15	3.96
Market 2	6.39	8.23	7.31	6.95	7.77	7.36	5.56	7.42	6.49	5.22	7.62	6.42

Price/Ton	Qtr 1 ($)			Qtr 2 ($)			Qtr 3 ($)			Qtr 4 ($)		
Bolt B	1	2	Avg	1	2	Avg	1	2	Avg	1	2	Avg
Market 1	4.33	4.34	4.33	3.94	4.04	3.99	4.29	3.47	3.88	2.77	5.15	3.96
Market 2	6.39	8.23	7.31	6.95	7.77	7.36	5.56	7.42	6.49	5.22	7.62	6.42

Instead of the complex mess of numbers above, Exhibit 5.2 presents the full pricing picture in a straightforward fashion.

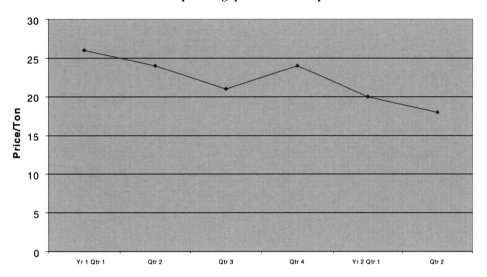

EXHIBIT 5.2   Pricing Trends

Downward pricing pressure on products

EXHIBIT 5.3   Marketplace Analysis

- Decreased widget consumption by customers has increased the volume of widgets in the metro area
- Consumption has decreased by 65%, which equates to approximately 550,000 units
- Widget prices have softened significantly as a result
- Widget commodity prices have been reduced by as much as 45%
- Metro area is now a net supplier of widgets
- Import activity put a lot of secondary volume on the market last year
- So far this year import activity is not at the same level as last year
- Customers are struggling to deliver orders to receive payments. This is not a significant market driver. Age of machines is a factor.

What the manager is really saying is shown in the Exhibit below.

EXHIBIT 5.4   Marketplace Analysis

Supply exceeds demand and pricing is under significant pressure

- ## Do not forget that the Marketing Plan template is directional
Think carefully about what the section is asking of you, do not treat the template as a checklist.   For example, Section 4 (Competitive Analysis) asks for a lot of information on your competitors.   However, when you think about it, this section is only asking you to identify two things: One, what are your competitors doing to take business away from you and, two, what you need to be doing to become a more formidable competitor.

- ## Spend a lot of time on Section 6 (Assessment of opportunities, threats, strengths, weaknesses and key issues)
The tendency when you develop your Plan is to spend more time on data collection and less time on data analysis.   This is flawed.   You will feel good about your effort ("I spent a lot of time on the Plan, boy, was it hard work!") but your Plan will be superficial.

Instead of working hard, I suggest you work smart.

As you are collecting your data for each section (and subjecting it to the litmus test I spoke of earlier), keep thinking about the implications for running your business and becoming a more effective competitor.

Data collection is easy, data analysis and synthesis is hard, it gives people a headache.   But, think about it like this – if all we had to do to succeed in the world of business was to collect data, all your competitors would be succeeding!

The world of business does not work in this way. Rewards go to those who can transform data into insight about the way they should be running their business. I want *you* to be such a person!

•   Ensure your strategies match the data

I will sometimes read a Marketing Plan where there is little connection between the data and the strategies. This happens when the strategies have been conceived independent of the data.

•   Ensure that your understanding of customer needs is not superficial

If your understanding of customer needs is superficial, I guarantee your plans will be superficial also. Recognize that understanding customer needs is not easy, you have to use some of the techniques (e.g., Value Chain Analysis and Total Cost of Ownership Analysis) I suggest in Chapter 4, Chapter 6, and Appendix 3.

•   Educate your organization on developing strategic Marketing Plans

A Marketing Plan should be a liberating document, not an enslaving one. Unfortunately, I come across many organizations where developing Plans is viewed with a jaundiced eye by managers. This is common because these managers have not been taught about the value of developing Plans. Therefore, the planning process is viewed as something additional or on top of what a manager does day to day.

"But, Ajay, I have a day job," is a statement I often hear from managers who have been asked to develop and run their businesses via plans. Essentially, what these managers are saying is this, "I really do not see the value in developing a plan." This is because they have not been *shown* the value. The planning component is imposed on them without any training.

"I have better things to do than develop a Marketing Plan." This statement was made by a manager when asked why his business was not developing Plans. His viewpoint is more troublesome because not only does he not view the Plan development as useful, he would rather run his business on the basis of fighting fires or crisis management.

My recommendation is to educate your employees on the value of running their business via Plan development. Start with some basic training and continually reinforce the central message that, from now on, this is the way the business is going to be run. Remember, successful businesses do not succeed by accident.

> Successful businesses earn their rewards in the marketplace by…
>
> ➤ Disciplined data collection
> ➤ Insight generation
> ➤ Superior strategy formulation
> ➤ Strategy execution
> ➤ Feedback and learning

• **Remind people that Marketing is everyone's job**

The Marketing Plan is the foundation upon which all other planning efforts are built. These include our Operating Plans and other plans such as sales and customer strategies. Every employee, regardless of functional affiliation, has a crucial role to play in the development and implementation of the Marketing Plan. This is because although the Plan may be put together by the Marketing Department it will not succeed unless everyone follows the guidelines set forth in the Plan in daily efforts to create value for customers.

• **Make Marketing Plan development part of a manager's scorecard**

What gets measured gets acted upon. I have come to realize that if you want to change the culture of your organization to one of a culture of discipline, you have to change behaviors first.

A client of mine illustrates the process of educating and evaluating business leaders on the merits of Marketing Plan development. They started by developing a standard Marketing Plan template that would be used by all their nine businesses. The Marketing Plans developed the first year were not perfect, but they were a start.

All businesses were given feedback on their Plans, training, and told what needed to be done to develop a more superior Plan the next year.

By year three, no longer were business leaders being evaluated on the structure of the Marketing Plans, but on the *content*. The thinking being drilled into the businesses constantly was – superior Plans mean superior results.

They even began documenting the differences between businesses in terms of performance. Clearly, businesses with superior Plans were turning in superior results. This, in turn, reinforced the need to run their business via Marketing Plans.

> **Adopt a patient attitude toward Marketing Plan development. Continuous learning and improvement is key!**

- **Do not forget it takes courage to develop and implement superior Marketing Plans**

Marketing planning forces you to make tradeoffs between business choices and, in this way, enables you to allocate your resources wisely. For example, the process of segmenting your customers may reveal to you that a portion of them should not be served because they are either unprofitable or marginally profitable. What do you do with this finding? It takes courage to be the person who makes the decision (or recommendation) to cut out a portion of your customer base.

Chapter 6

Marketing Planning to Sales Execution: Sales and Key Account (Customer) Plans

In This Chapter You Will Find…

➢ How businesses make the transition from Marketing planning to Sales execution

➢ The role of the Sales function in Marketing Led – Sales Driven businesses
  ➢ From "selling" to "customer relationship management"

➢ Relationship between Sales Plans and Key Account (Customer) Plans

➢ How to develop Sales Plans
  ➢ A Sales Plan template

➢ How to develop a Key Account (Customer) Plan
  ➢ A Key Account (Customer) Plan template

Let us make the transition from Marketing planning to Sales execution. To do this, recall the exhibit from Chapter 1, reproduced below.

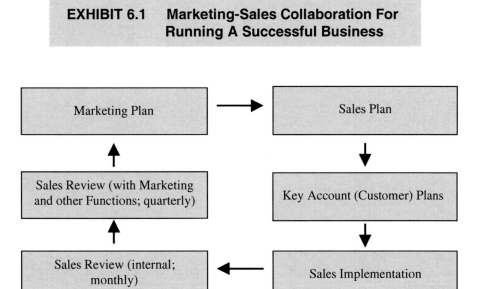

EXHIBIT 6.1   Marketing-Sales Collaboration For Running A Successful Business

What you should see from the Exhibit is this – to understand-create-deliver and manage customer value, Marketing, Sales, and other Functions within the business have to work as *one* team. Each function brings its expertise to the table and, working together, they win in the marketplace (I will have more to say about the role of other functions in the next chapter. Let us focus on Marketing and Sales in this chapter).

What value has Marketing created up to this point (with the help of Sales and other functions; details are presented in the next chapter)? To answer this question we need to recall the Marketing Plan template from Chapter 3.

Up to this point Marketing has...

- Conducted an external analysis of the markets we compete in, competitors we face and analyzed segments (markets and customers) we serve in terms of needs, trends and attractiveness.
- Coupled the external analysis with an internal analysis to identify key opportunities and threats facing the business. When examined alongside our key strengths and weaknesses, these key opportunities and threats revealed a set of key issues we must address.
- Identified objectives, strategies and tactics by segments.
- Provided a clear justification for chosen strategies in terms of how they will garner a competitive advantage for us vis-à-vis our competitors.
- Made clear how the Marketing – Sales linkage will take place by developing segment-level value propositions.
- Identified target customers within each segment.
- Told us how much money we will make if we implement and control the Marketing Plan successfully.

This is great, don't you think? Marketing has shown us where to fish in a large pool of water for maximum success. It is up to the Sales function now to go and do the fishing, report on conditions and success, and meet with Marketing to learn from implementation efforts so the process shown in the Exhibit can start all over again next year.

As you can see, the role of the Sales function shifts from "selling" to something else. As one wise author put it, the role of Marketing is to make selling superfluous. Notice, it says to make "selling" superfluous, not to make the Sales function superfluous. In fact, Sales takes on a heightened role in a Marketing Led – Sales Driven organization. The Sales force becomes, in the words of one business leader, Customer Relationship Managers, managing the customer base (current and future) for long-term mutually profitable relationships.

| In a Marketing Led – Sales Driven business the role of Sales shifts... ||
From	*To*
Negotiating for the customer's business	Creating customer value
Having expert product knowledge	Having expertise about the customer's business and industry
Supplying the customer with product and market information	Helping the customer grow their business
Selling a product	Delivering value
Identifying customer problems	Consultative customer solutions
Volume planning with customer	Building a business plan in partnership with the customer
Salesperson-customer focus	Senior management (supplier)-senior management (customer) focus
Sales function focus	Total involvement of all functions
Focus on many customers	Focus on few attractive customers

For Marketing and Sales to work seamlessly with each other, the Marketing Plan gets translated into a Sales Plan, which provides the direction for the development of Key Account Plans and Customer Plans (I am going to use these terms interchangeably; a Key Account Plan is a Customer Plan, albeit for a key account or customer). This is shown in Exhibit 6.2.

EXHIBIT 6.2   Marketing Plans to Sales Execution

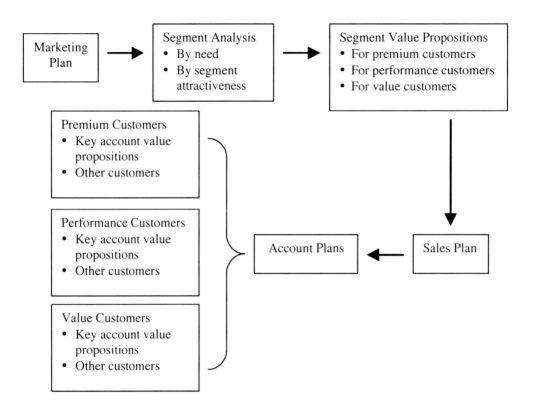

Do not forget that I use the terms "Premium", "Performance", and "Value" for illustration purposes only. You may choose to categorize your customers using other nomenclature.

In the next chapter I show you how the translation from Marketing Plans to Sales Plans takes place. I even provide an annual planning calendar you can use.

In this chapter, let us see what a Sales Plan and Key Account Plan templates look like. Before we do this, let us examine the relationship between Sales Plans and Key Account (Customer) Plans. This relationship is shown in Exhibit 6.3.

EXHIBIT 6.3   Relationship Between Sales Plans and Key Account Plans

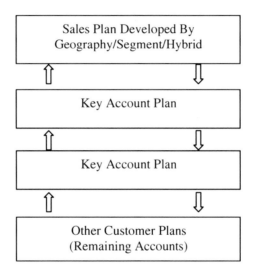

As can be seen from the Exhibit, the business develops a Sales Plan, which can be developed by geography or segments or industry verticals (according to how the sales territory is defined in the business; some businesses divide the entire market by geography, while others divide it by segments). I have also seen businesses develop Sales Plans that are a hybrid between geography and segment (e.g., large customers in the East or pharmaceutical, HBA and institutional customers located in the South).

The Sales Plan provides the common direction (context setting) for the development of two other plans: Key Account Plans and Other Customer Plans. But, as can be seen from Exhibit 6.3, the Key Account Plans also get rolled up into the Sales Plan, thus ensuing a collaborative nature between these two types of plans. As I will show in the next chapter, as the Key Account and Customer Plans are being implemented during the year, the Sales function meets monthly to review implementation and make any adjustments to the Sales Plan.

Developing The Sales Plan

Important: Sales Plans are developed by geography, segment or a hybrid model. I am assuming the business has made decisions regarding how the sales force will be deployed (geography, segment or hybrid) *before* the Sales Plan is developed.

The main purpose of the Sales Plan is to:
➤ Support corporate strategic objectives by building on the direction and context provided by the Marketing Plan
➤ Provide a common direction and context for the development of Key Account and Customer Plans[16]

I have not provided a separate "Owner's Manual" for the Sales Plan template as the details on how to use the Marketing Plan template (Chapter 4) also apply to the Sales Plan.

As you will see upon reading the template below, many details regarding the Sales Plan are directly lifted from the Marketing Plan. This is how it should be – Sales and Marketing collaborating with each other to plan-implement-learn-plan.

---

[16] Notice that just as the Marketing Plan provided the context for the development of other Functional Plans (e.g., Sales, Production, etc.), the Sales Plan provides the context for development of Key Account and other Customer Plans.

Exhibit 6.4 Sales Plan Template

Section 1. Executive Summary
- Key sales issues facing the business
- Key sales opportunities
- Key sales objectives and outcomes
- Key sales strategies
- Key resources required

Section 2. Table of Contents

Section 3. Opportunity Analysis
- Our historical performance in segment or geography
- Market, customer, product and competitor analysis
- Top issues and opportunities in this segment or geography
- Target customers by priority
- Target prospects by priority

Section 4. Performance Targets
- Positioning relative to competition
- Volume targets by market segment/geography
- Revenue targets by market segment/geography
- Market share targets by segment/geography
- Profitability targets by market segment/geography
- Other

Section 5. Sales Strategies
- Value propositions by market segment
- Value propositions by customer
- Products
- Profitable mix
- Pricing
- Marketing communications
- New business development
- Supply chain
- Sales force deployment
- Sales organization effectiveness
- Other

Section 6. Sales Plan Implementation and Control
- Detailed tactical plans for each Sales strategy
- Detailed control plans to monitor Sales execution

Section 7. Sales Budgets and Key Resources
- Budgets
- Resource requirements

An example of a Sales Plan is presented in Appendix 2.

Developing Key Account Plans

In Exhibit 6.5 I present a detailed template to develop Key Account (Customer) Plans[17]. A Key Account Plan has two parts, one is a Key Account Profile (sections 1 – 6) and the other is a Key Account Sales Plan (section 7).

The Key Account Profile (updated yearly) enables us to profile our customer and make a decision regarding our customer (Is this customer still an attractive customer? Should we continue targeting this customer as a "key" customer?). The Key Account Sales Plan outlines details regarding what objectives we want to achieve with this customer, what actions we want to take, who will do what by when, what metrics we will use to monitor progress and other details such as contingency plans.

An example of a Key Account Plan is presented in Appendix 3.

---

[17] A Key Account (Customer) Plan may be developed for a *single* customer (for example, Wal-Mart) or for a *group* of customers (for example, a business may develop a Customer Plan for the Small Business segment, which could potentially include millions of customers).

Exhibit 6.5 Key Account Plan Template[18]

Section 1. Customer Description
- Location
- What business
- Structure and ownership
- Operations and brands
- Customer mission and values
- Other pertinent information (e.g., names of company officers, number of employees, website, etc.)

Section 2. Customer Performance
- Our product sales history with customer and trends; vs. competition
- Our performance vs. goals
- Claims
- Trip reports
- Visits to our company (dates/who/locations, etc.)
- Visits to customer (dates/who/locations, etc.)

Section 3. Customer Buying Process
- Who makes buying decisions?
- How are buying decisions made?
  - Buying patterns (customer buying trends)
  - Buying process (how decisions are made)
  - Primary contact (buyer)
  - Degree of authority in conducting purchases, supplier programs, customer programs
  - Other key personnel that may impact or enhance a value proposition (e.g., gatekeepers, influencers, etc.)
  - Any history with our company that may help or hinder value creation
- Top buying decision criteria? How do we compare with our competitors?

---

[18] Remember, as with the other templates (for Marketing Plans and Sales Plans), do not treat the bullet points under each section as a checklist. Understand clearly why the section is there and what it is asking of you in terms of data.

Section 4. Customer Needs[19]

- How does the customer want our product delivered?[20]
  - Quantities
  - Terms and conditions
  - Delivery
  - Invoicing
  - Rebates
  - Special terms
  - Vendor Managed Inventory (VMI)
  - Just In Time Delivery (JIT)
  - Other
- What activities does customer complete before and after purchase of product? What activities does the customer have to do to Acquire, Possess, Use and Dispose of our product?[21]
  - Can we quantify (dollar value) these activities?
- What does the customer use the product for?
- Can we increase customer revenue or decrease customer cost?
- What does customer need help with when they use our product?
  - Any unmet needs, current and in the future?
- Is our product the customer's ultimate need, or are there other needs?
  - Is our product fabricated for other uses?
- Strategic direction being pursued by customer
  - How can we help?
- Customer business priorities for next year
- What market segments does customer serve?

---

[19] In this section, do not be concerned if you do not have all the information about the customer in order to profile your customer's needs. Treat your knowledge gap as an opportunity to learn about your customer's needs. **Remember this – your only source of long-term competitive advantage is your ability to understand the needs of your customers faster and in a superior fashion to your competitors.**

[20] Together, these items are referred to as Service Level Agreements (SLAs). These are items that you have contracted with the customer.

[21] This is called Total Cost of Ownership (TCO) Analysis. Its intention is to enable us to reduce our customer's total cost of doing business with us. The idea being that, if we are successful in reducing our customer's total cost of ownership, our customer would be more willing to consider paying a price premium for our product. TCO Analysis is a good way to understand customer needs, without having to ask them. More details on this in the Key Account Plan example in Appendix 3.

- Current
- Future (how can we assist?)
- How does our customer create value for his customer?
  - What needs do their customers have that are not being currently met?

Section 5. Customer SWOT Analysis

- Customer's competitors (provide details)
- Alternate product competition (example, wood versus steel)
- Major opportunities and threats facing customer
- Customer's strengths and weaknesses to respond to opportunities and threats
- How can we help customer compete more effectively?
- Top 3 business problems to be solved for customer?

Section 6. Key Account Analysis

- Customer marketplace performance
- Customer financial health
- Current and historical relationship between customer and our company
- How important is this customer to us?
- Is there compatibility between customer and us?
- Does this customer fit our segmentation and value proposition strategy?
- How does customer view suppliers?
- How are suppliers treated?
- Are they willing to partner with us in value creation efforts?
- Unmet customer needs based on above information
  - Can we quantify unmet needs?
  - Can we satisfy unmet needs?
  - Do we have the resources?
- Customer opportunities (for us) and quantification of economic value to us
- Current customer profit level to our company
- Future customer profit potential (customer attractiveness) based on above information
- Customer profit gap (profit gap = future customer profit potential – current customer profit level to our company)
- What value will we need to create in order to close profit gap?
  - What is our cost to serve (create value)?
- *What is our decision regarding customer? Reasons for the decision?*

Section 7. Key Account Sales Plan

- Account objectives
- Key actions to be taken with customer
- Value propositions to be developed
- Key steps to be taken to create, deliver and manage value propositions
- Success metrics
- Timing of steps
- Responsibilities/accountabilities assigned
- Resources required
- Control of Key Account Plan
- Linkage to Marketing and other plans (Sales, Production, etc.)
- Risk involved, competitor response, contingency plans
- Action plan status

Chapter 7

An Annual Planning Calendar For Achieving Cross-Functional Alignment

In This Chapter You Will Find...

➤ How "driving – market" organizations align all functions so they are all working toward a common set of goals

➤ Detailed annual planning calendar to align functions in any organization
  ➤ Development of Marketing Plan phase 1
  ➤ Cross-functional review
  ➤ Development of Marketing Plan phase 2
  ➤ Cross-functional review
  ➤ Development of Sales and Customer Plans
  ➤ Development of other Functional Plans
  ➤ Final budget approval
  ➤ Implementation and on-going review of plans so the plan-implement-learn-plan cycle operates smoothly

Cross-functional Planning For Success

We have seen that in successful business organizations, Marketing and Sales work together to create, implement and evaluate marketplace strategies. How does this lyrical dance take place, exactly? And, not just between Marketing and Sales, but with other functions as well? After all, in a well-oiled and smoothly functioning business, there are other crucial functions such as Production, Finance, Supply Chain, Human Resources, Customer Service that must participate and work alongside Marketing and Sales for success.

Consider a "simple" exercise as setting the price for a business' products. In shortsighted organizations this step is done by one function (say, Marketing or Finance) in isolation of other functions. This is a mistake because strategic price setting depends upon several factors including:

* Our cost to produce
* The customers' perception of product value and the price they are willing to pay
* An acceptable return on investment
* Our ability to produce more efficiently (and thereby cut our costs of production) based on an assessment of what customers are willing to pay
* Marketplace factors such as competitors' prices and economic conditions

Smart organizations, on the other hand, incorporate price considerations not only in their product development process, but even early on when the product is still in the concept stage. As you can appreciate, such orchestration requires the active participation of all functions in a business.

> **"Driving-market" business organizations (notice, I did not say "market-driven", which to me is a reactive organization) achieve alignment between different functions using an annual planning calendar.**
>
> **As a result, the entire business achieves total customer focus by knowing what key issues are important and what strategies will be in place to win in the marketplace.**

Without an annual planning calendar different parts of the business tend to move in different directions, each focused exclusively on acting in the best interests of *their* function, regardless of the consequences for the health of the entire business organization.

A story from a client of mine illustrates this point perfectly. In spite of Marketing insisting that customers desired 10-inch widgets (based on a thorough understanding of customer needs), the Production function produced 12-inch widgets. Why? Because by producing 12-inch widgets, the factory ran more efficiently and raw material was utilized with less waste. To make matters worse, the plant manager was measured and compensated, not on customer satisfaction, but on how efficiently he ran his factory.

As a result, customers had to cut 2 inches from the product to use it in their factories. Customers were saying all along that they would pay more for 10-inch widgets because this would save them money from lost time and additional labor. However, it did not matter because the Production function operated in its own silo.

How was the problem ultimately resolved? The senior management of the business vowed to operate as a cross-functional enterprise, and put in place a planning calendar along the lines shown in Exhibit 7.1.

In Exhibit 7.1 I present an annual planning calendar you can use to ensure that all parts of your business are functioning as one, customer-focused, enterprise, and not as a collection of silos operating in the interests of their own functions alone.

As you can tell, Exhibit 7.1 is essentially Exhibit 3.1 with timelines added to it.

**EXHIBIT 7.1   Cross-Functional Alignment For Running
A Successful Business**

Step	Description	Timing
Business Strategic Plan Direction	3 – 5 year document, updated yearly	On-going[22]
Marketing Plan Phase 1 (Sections 1 – 7) Developed by the Marketing function	External and internal analysis, key issues to be addressed by the business and objectives to be achieved next year Sent to other functions (e.g., production, sales, finance, supply chain, customer service) for their review	April 1
Cross-Functional Meeting	Meeting of all functional heads to discuss and approve Marketing Plan Phase 1 assumptions, analysis, key issues to be addressed by the business At this point, all functions in complete alignment on key business issues and objectives to be achieved Functions start to work on their own plans	Early June
Marketing Plan Phase 2 (Sections 8 – 15) Developed by the Marketing function	Strategies, tactics and key outcomes for next year Sent to functions so they can review and modify their own plans, as necessary	September 1
Cross-Functional Meeting	Meeting of cross-functional heads to discuss and approve Marketing Plan Phase 2 strategies and tactics	Early October
Sales and Key Account Plans Developed	Sales and Key Account Plans developed and approved	October
Functional Plans Developed	Other Functional Plans (e.g., production) developed and approved	October - November
Final budgets approved	Business approves final budgets	November - December
Implementation of Sales Plans	Implementation of Key Account and Customer Plans. This is where the rubber meets the road.	Ongoing
On-going Review of Plans	• Sales organization meets internally monthly to discuss Key Account and Customer Plans execution • Sales meets with Marketing and other Functions quarterly to discuss Sales execution, functional alignment and corrective actions	• Monthly • Quarterly

---

[22] The business' corporate Strategic Plan is like the Queen Mary 2, moving along from New York to Southhampton. It does not change its course lightly. The Strategic Plan's main purpose is to provide the entire business with a sense of direction.

What does Exhibit 7.1 tell us? Firstly, the Business' Strategic Plan (review this material in Chapter 3, if necessary) provides on-going guidance to the entire business throughout the year.

As we saw in Chapter 3, the Marketing Plan is a one-year slice of the Strategic Plan. But, as we also have discussed, the Marketing Function cannot develop a Marketing Plan in isolation of other functions and simply hand them the Marketing Plan to implement. The planning calendar in Exhibit 7.1 illustrates the collaborative nature of Marketing Plan development.

It is for this reason the Marketing function develops what I call a Marketing Plan Phase 1, which essentially is sections 1 through 7 of the Marketing Plan. This document presents an analysis of:

- The external and internal environment facing the business
- Key issues the business must address the next year (and following years, as necessary)
- Objectives that must be achieved next year in the segments the business operates in (or new markets the business should be entering)

The Marketing Plan Phase 1 is developed by April 1 and Marketing sends it to the other functions for their review. So, the Marketing function has taken the steward role in doing the initial analysis (based on input from other functions and input from implementation of plans from last year) for the other functions to consider.

In early June cross-functional team members[23] gather for a 1-day planning session in which they discuss the assumptions underlying Marketing Plan Phase 1, analysis, key issues and objectives. The cross-functional team makes adjustments as necessary and the meeting adjourns. Notice what happens at the end of this session:

At the end of the 1-day session on Marketing Plan Phase 1, *all* functions should be in complete alignment about what key issues impact the business and what needs to be accomplished next year. At this point, all functions are marching toward the same set of goals. Also, each function now begins to work on its *own* functional plan because it knows what it needs to do to accomplish the objectives jointly approved by the cross-functional team.

---

[23] This team is called by different names in business organizations – Joint Team, Lead Team, etc.

Based on input from other functions, Marketing develops the complete Marketing Plan (Phase 2) by September 1 and sends it to the functions for their review. Marketing Plan Phase 2, of course, outlines the key strategies, tactics and key outcomes expected for next year.

In early October, the cross-functional team meets again to discuss the complete Marketing Plan and approve strategies and tactics. During October, the Sales function develops its Sales and Key Account Plans. By November (at the latest) all functional plans have been developed and approved. The business develops and approves final budgets by the November – December time period.

The enterprise is now ready for business for the next year. There is still the month of December for any adjustments as necessary.

Next year, as the different plans are being implemented, it is the Sales function that is the business' eyes and ears in the marketplace. Key Account and Customer Plans are the litmus test of how well the business has synthesized external and internal issues and developed strategies to create value for the customer.

Therefore, it is vital that we not wait until the end of the year to see how well the implementation went. Rather, the Sales function meets internally every month to review Sales implementation and meets at least every quarter with Marketing and the other cross-functional members to discuss Sales execution, make any adjustments and ensure continued complete alignment between the functions.

I started this book by saying that success in the competitive world of business is not accidental. I hope you have seen how driving-market businesses work together to synthesize data, develop strategies, implement initiatives, and review and learn from their marketplace execution. In my experience, it is the focus on these fundamentals that ensures their success. Done year in and year out, this fundamental activity will ensure the long-term success of any enterprise.

Appendix 1

Marketing Plan Example

Executive Summary[24]

Internal and external analysis of our markets identified several key business issues we must address next year:

➢ Need to address the threat of substitutes (plastics) taking share away from us
➢ Leverage product innovation to address customer needs such as flexible manufacturing and high impact packaging
➢ Develop strategies with select group of Widget customers to build contract business
➢ Continue to leverage premium pricing strategy by lowering customer total cost in use and helping our customers penetrate new markets

Based on these key issues, we have a plan to achieve $1.34 billion sales and $295 million EBIT[25] through sales of 32,000,000 units, and increase market share by 4.1% next year by introducing new products, reducing costs and flawless execution of Sales Plans based on Marketing strategies.

We have established the following objectives for next year:

➢ Achieve $1.34 billion sales and $295 million EBIT through sales of 32,000,000 units, and increase market share by 4.1% next year
➢ Introduce 7 new products contributing $155 million sales and $30 million EBIT
➢ Strengthen our position with customers and improve our perception with prospects by improving top box ratings of customer satisfaction survey by 15%
➢ Grow international business to receive 5% share and 1,250,000 units resulting in sales of $140 million and generating $28 million EBIT
➢ Provide support to sales force in translating marketing strategies into actionable Sales Plans by developing more compelling value propositions to our customers, resulting in an increase of Premium customers by 30%

---

[24] Please note that all numbers are for illustrative purposes only. Do not try to do arithmetic computations on them to match figures.
[25] Earnings Before Interest and Taxes

In order to achieve our objectives we must focus on four key strategies

➢ **Product Strategy**
Create value-added products for pharmaceutical, food and multi-media markets, and leverage total cost in use including machine utilization flexibility for food and general consumer markets

➢ **Pricing Strategy**
Continue to support premium pricing strategy by delivering superior value in goods and services (web apps and sample program) to target customers

➢ **Channel Strategy**
Continue building relationships with key accounts while beginning to develop relationships with target companies in target segments including manufacturing, pharmaceuticals, food, multi-media and general consumer

➢ **Marketing/Communication Strategy**
Strengthen our position with customers and improve our perception with prospects

Successful implementation of the tactics supporting the strategies listed above will benefit the business in several critical areas:

➢ Broadened product line supporting key customer needs
➢ Increased competitiveness and exposure in international markets
➢ Increased insight into specific customer needs and value chain
➢ Advanced data based selling programs leveraging customer total cost in use
➢ Continued segmentation and development of specific value propositions
➢ Executable and actionable Sales Plans developed from this Marketing Plan
➢ Improved communications to strengthen perception with prospects

Table of Contents

---

[26] Page numbers seen here are for illustration purposes only.

Widget Business Overview					
Product Line	**Current Year Sales ($Million)**	**Market Share**	**5-Yr. Average ROI**	**5-Yr. Average EBIT ($ Million)**	**Current Year Capital Employed ($Million)**
ABC	$350	15%	22%	$85	$100
KLM	$110	32%	15%	$37	$50
XYZ	$185	10%	7%	$26	$55
DEF	$55	5%	4%	$7	$72
GHI	$250	40%	17%	$45	$173
Total	**$950**	**30%**	**15.2%**	**$200**	**$450**
Our DEF product line continues to under perform, based on minimum ROI expectations of 7%.					

KEY INITIATIVES FROM LAST YEAR AND LESSONS LEARNED			
Initiative	**Goal**	**Status**	**Lessons Learned**
Segment customers by need and profitability	Q2	Completed	This is the key to our success as we face increasing numbers of low-priced competitors. Currently, we have categorized our customers into Premium, Performance and Value. Opportunities exist to refine our segmentation scheme as we move forward
Resize machine at Bloomfield plant	Q4	Completed, but we encountered problems with product quality	Customer communication is key. We must develop contingency plans as we resize machines in our other operations
Conduct a formal customer satisfaction survey	Q3	Completed	Although we scored well, we must continually create value for our customers
Implement premium pricing model across targeted segments	Q2	Completed	We lost business to lower priced competitors. However, our strategic Plan is very clear about our direction – we do not want to serve customers who are price sensitive but demand high levels of resources from us
Implement sales tracking tools	Q3	Completed	Superior sales tracking by sales person, plant, segment, customer and product has enabled us to add $15 million EBIT last year. We need to rollout this tool to all market segments in which we operate

Marketplace Analysis

Global expansion as well as large Manufacturers, Mass Merchants and Home Centers will play a key role in our strategies

Summary of Key Facts
- Global Widget market is 150 billion units with projected 4% annual market growth
- Increased pressure from alternative products such as plastics
- Internationally there are different product requirements
- Capacity growth in Asia, especially in BXC
- Higher visual appeal packaging requirements
- Supplier consolidation by customers
- Fewer and bigger customers
- Dominant retailers exert more control over our customers

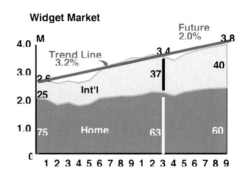

Widget Market

Source: Business Trends.

Implications
- Limited alternative manufacturing capabilities lessen our ability to grow share globally
- Consolidation through the entire value chain is driving the need for us to reduce total cost of products and services
- Current product offering limits our ability to compete globally due to stiffness, yield, and needs to be addressed
- New strategy in Europe needs to be implemented
- Due to major retailer dominance, effective merchandising will continue to be a critical component of product pull, thus requiring better, more technologically advanced packaging
- Need to analyze internal systems and measurements to better address product quality issues

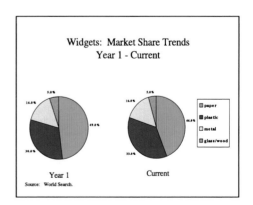

Widgets: Market Share Trends
Year 1 - Current

Channel of Distribution Trends

Key Facts:

- Channel dynamics continue to change as customers explore different channel options in an effort to become more efficient.
- Distributors are fighting to keep share and struggling to justify the true value that they offer in the supply chain.
- Printers are signing long-term supply agreements with key customers. Also, their contracts have punitive damage for material supplied by other distribution channels.
- Increasingly, large volume customers want a direct relationship with manufacturers.
- Distributor margins and receivables are under tremendous pressure.
- Customer-driven relationships facilitate solution selling and enable the creation of switching barriers.

Implications:

- In addition to providing value directly to end users, we must partner with major channel members to protect our share.
- We must make financial stability a key focus for next year.

Pricing Trends

Market Price Trend for Widgets

Key Observations

- From Year 1 through current year pricing has gained ground from the lowest levels
- Pricing trend appears to be stabilizing at $700/unit
- We foresee this trend to continue

Implications

- Customer segmentation that began 2 years ago contributed to our ability to hold pricing
- Downtime, plant closings and other measures were taken to manage our capacity versus demand
- Strategy going forward should focus on eliminating downtime and maximizing profit by concentrating on most appropriate product and customer mix while leveraging value to support premium pricing

Marketplace Analysis: Summary of Business Implications

➤ Address threat of plastic taking share from away from us
  ➤ Develop widget materials to better compete with plastics
  ➤ Promote our material as a renewable, more environmentally friendly alternative
➤ Stronger focus on innovation
  ➤ Superior printability material and other value-add liners for higher impact packaging
➤ Need for different product offering for international markets
  ➤ Yield, stiffness, shade, brightness, etc.
➤ Continue customer segmentation and offer stronger value propositions to strengthen relationships with target customers
  ➤ We should focus on the right customer and product mix
➤ Need optimized selling and manufacturing strategy in international markets
  ➤ Production in Asia and Europe
  ➤ Value propositions for select customers
  ➤ Stronger relationships with agents
➤ We need to better manage capacity versus demand
  ➤ We need to think of forming a supply – demand allocation function
➤ Need to address global market dynamics as product and packaging move to low cost regions
  ➤ Better competitive intelligence
➤ Improve supply chain efficiencies through programs such as VMI, JIT, Internet tracking and on-time delivery
➤ Need to analyze internal systems and measurements to better address customer product quality issues

Competitive Analysis: Business Implications
Competitors' consolidation and increased level of integration continues to bring challenges to our industry. Lower priced competitors will continue to make inroads. (Please see appendix for detailed profiles on individual competitors.)

➤ Need for better competitive intelligence
➤ Focus on selected retail segments and relationships with target companies in those segments
  ➤ Total solutions team concept
  ➤ Discovering and capturing met and unmet customer needs
  ➤ Speed to market of new products

➢ Address product quality issues against competitors capable of offering M3X technology
➢ Need for different product offering for international markets
  ➢ Yield, stiffness, shade, brightness, etc.
➢ Need to address competitive issues with external business versus internal divisions
➢ Focused sales effort on stronger value propositions to address target and positioning of STP
➢ Selling strategy on value-added features to compete with price-cutting competition such as:
  ➢ Superior machine performance
  ➢ Trouble free raw material utilization
  ➢ Improved technical and service offerings

Segmentation Analysis: Markets and Customers

We operate primarily in three market segments: Pharmaceutical, Manufacturing, and Food. Multi Media and Global are new markets for us. The analysis below identifies trends and needs in each of these segments. (We used Value Chain Analysis to accurately understand customer needs).

MARKET SEGMENT REVIEW					
	Pharma	**Manufc.**	**Food**	**Multi Media**	**Global**
Growth rate	7%	4%	10%	15%	22%
Pricing outlook (5 Yr.)	$150/unit	$120	$320	$175	$205
Our share	25%	43%	20%	0	5%
Profitability	Average	Average	Above avg.	Well above avg.	Well above avg.
Segment attractiveness	Average	Medium	High	High	High
Strategic fit	High	Medium	High	High	High
Segment decision	Maintain	Maintain	Grow	Grow	Grow
Multi media and global are new segments for us. As indicated above, our analysis reveals that they are very attractive segments and we must pursue them aggressively. Currently, we have not segmented the global market along the lines of our domestic market. This is a step that will be pursued in the future.					

PRODUCT LINE SALES TO SEGMENTS

Product Line	Pharma (million units and $ million annual)		Manufc. (million units and $ million annual)		Food (million units and $ million annual)		Total	
ABC	1.6	$150	2.5	$200	---	---	4.1	$350
KLM	3.2	$40	0.6	$40	1.7	$30	5.5	$110
XYZ	---	---	1.3	$140	2.2	$45	3.5	$185
DEF	0.25	$12	0.95	$43	---	---	1.2	$55
GHI	1.46	$125	2.0	$83	5.1	$42	8.56	$250

We currently do not offer our ABC line in the Food segment. Our analysis has revealed Food to be growing at 10% annually. Therefore, we should think about how we can secure channels of distribution for the ABC line in this segment.

The XYZ line is not offered currently in the Pharma market segment. However, our analysis indicates that we should not pursue this opportunity at the present time. Instead, resources should be devoted to penetrating the multi media segment, a growth opportunity for us.

The DEF product line is best represented in the manufacturing segment. Our decision with this segment is to maintain our presence. Currently, we serve the manufacturing segment with all of our product lines. Our analysis reveals that we should phase out the DEF line within the next 5 years.

PRODUCT LINE REVIEW

Product Line	Current Year Sales ($Million)	Market Share	5-Yr. Average ROI	5-Yr. Average EBIT ($ Million)	Current Year Capital Employed ($Million)
ABC	$350	15%	22%	$85	$100
KLM	$110	32%	15%	$37	$50
XYZ	$185	10%	7%	$26	$55
DEF	$55	5%	4%	$7	$72
GHI	$250	40%	17%	$45	$173
Total	**$950**	**30%**	**15.2%**	**$200**	**$450**

Our DEF product line continues to under perform, based on minimum ROI expectations of 7%.

Pharma Segment Trends[27]

- Aging baby boomer population and increased longevity is impacting the strong growth (7%) in this segment.
- Consumers are increasingly health conscious and are taking charge of their personal health choices.
- Last year this market generated $350 billion in global sales, with North America accounting for 48% and Europe 24%.
- Industry consolidation is expected to continue.
- Widget market for pharmaceuticals is estimated at 25 million units.
- This market segment accounted for 15% of EBIT last year.
- Next year we estimate this market segment to be even more attractive with 19% EBIT.

Pharma Segment Implications

- We need to build stronger relationships with our customers to penetrate this market.
- New product development will be key to success in this market place. Specifically, we see a need to develop products to capture the Direct To Consumer (DTC) marketing communications programs that major pharma companies have launched.

Based on customer **needs** and **attractiveness** to us, we have categorized our customers into three segments: Premium, Performance, Value.

Premium Customer Segment Description and Needs[28]

- These customers require proactive sales solutions and are willing to pay us a price premium.
- 24/7 technical support.
- Customer service desk.
- They want us to share with them research on market trends and end user trends and needs.
- New, innovative products to compete in the marketplace.
- No "stock outs".
- Special requests from warehousing to packaging.

---

[27] Only one market segment description is being provided here.
[28] Only two customer segment (Premium and Value) descriptions are being provided here.

Premium Customer Segment Implications

- We should actively develop this customer segment as it is the most attractive in terms of contracts, price premiums and our capabilities.
- Premium customers represent 20% of our sales revenues and 35% of our profits.
- Developing this customer segment will require us to invest in R&D, customer service and sales effectiveness.

Value Segment Trends and Needs

- Require basic product quality and product bundling options.
- Not willing to consider price premiums.
- Tend to be price sensitive and tend to switch suppliers.

Value Segment Implications

- We should continue to serve this customer segment as they enable us to utilize our excess capacity.
- Also, this customer segment is lucrative because they buy the basic product from us. Without this segment, we would have to consider selling the basic product at a deep discount.
- However, these customers should be increasingly served electronically so we reduce our cost to serve them.
- We should conduct a customer review every year and eliminate the least profitable 3% of our value customers.

The chart below identifies a market segment by customer segment matrix. Each cell in the matrix identifies a set of **needs**.

	Premium	**Performance**	**Value**
Pharma	• Highest-grade quality • Proactive technical support • Willing to pay price premiums	• Consistent product quality • System efficiencies • May consider price premiums if case is made	• Basic quality • Product bundling • Will not consider price premiums
Manufc.	• High-impact product • Proactive technical support • Willing to pay price premiums	• User friendly packages • Quick turnaround • May consider price premiums if case is made	• Consistency in product • Sales materials • Will not consider price premiums
Food	• Custom solutions • Security of supply • Willing to pay price premiums	• Cost containment • Security of supply • Will consider price premiums if case is made	• Diversified product line • Competitive price

CUSTOMER REVIEW[29]					
Customer Segment	**Customer**	**Sales ($ million)**	**Cost to Serve ($/unit)**	**Customer Profitability ($/unit)**	**Decision**
Premium	Belvedere Co.	$23	$12	$25	Grow
	Briar Co.	$42	$20	$15	Grow
	Cameron Co.	$100	$44	$4	Reduce cost to serve
	Deal Inc.	$15	$35	$17	Grow
	Real Co.	$5	$45	($20)	Negotiate contract for better terms or drop[30]
Performance	ABC Co.	$25	$25	$7	Shows signs of Value customer. Need further data to validate
	Bonyton Inc.	$11	$35	$12	Grow
	Bossier Ind.	$56	$26	$45	Potential to become Premium customer
	Catmatsu Co.	$78	$34	$23	Grow

[29] As you can see in this section, this business has taken a hard look at its customer base (only partially displayed here) to make decisions about who to grow with, which customers to maintain and which customers should be dropped. In my experience, smart businesses continually evaluate their customer base, dropping the least attractive customers on an annual basis.

[30] This hypothetical customer is based on a real example. A client of mine approached their customer to renegotiate their contract for better terms (this is because analysis revealed this customer to not be very profitable). The customer refused the terms suggested by my client and so the two of them parted ways. Three months later, the customer came back and agreed to the new terms.

What happened in the interim? The customer examined the benefits/price offered by my client's competitors and realized that my client's benefits/price ratio was higher. My client could say "no" to the customer in the first place because they had done the analysis and knew their cost to serve, the customer's needs and value drivers, and competitor offerings.

Without such analysis, when a customer says "jump", we say "how high"?

CUSTOMER REVIEW (continued)					
Customer Segment	**Customer**	**Sales ($ million)**	**Cost to Serve ($/unit)**	**Customer Profitability ($/unit)**	**Decision**
Value	Aim Co.	$34	$26	$17	Maintain
	Bruno Mfc.	$85	$11	$18	Maintain
	Caruthers Co.	$67	$15	$25	Potential to become Performance customer
	Eigen Mfc.	$12	$46	($15)	Reduce cost to serve or drop

Customer Satisfaction Survey: Key Findings

A customer satisfaction survey conducted last year identified the following:

- Our overall satisfaction score is 4.4 (out of 5). This compares very favorably with the competition.
- However, our loyalty rates are below our competitors'.
- On-time delivery continues to be a problem for us compared to the competition. We have managed a 87% on-time delivery rate versus 92% for the competition.
- Customer technical service agents need to improve product knowledge and problem diagnosis skills.
- Customers complain that our sales force needs to be more accessible and willing to listen to customer needs.

Assessment of Opportunities, Threats, Strengths, Weaknesses and Key Issues

Our Position
Current Market Share EST.: 30%   Capacity Utilization: 91.9%

Key Opportunities
- Develop and execute strong value propositions in select target segments
- Exploit Total Solutions Team concept with emerging customers
- Leverage overseas facilities and develop stronger value propositions and differentiated product offering to better compete in international markets
- Improve supply chain efficiencies

Key Threats
- Plastics taking share from our material
- Suppliers are expanding integration efforts
- Lower priced competitors are targeting our traditional markets
- European competition coming to North American market
- Competitive acquisitions offering stronger value propositions

Key Strengths
- Large capacity
- Manufacturing flexibility
- Strong technology resources
- Cost competitive
- Staying power & consistency of supply
- Comprehensive product line offering
- Cross-functional expertise to create customer value

Key Weaknesses
- Domestic production only
- Machine resizing issues in XYZ line
- Incomplete product portfolio
- Operational excellence (on-time delivery) issues
- Incomplete competitive intelligence

Business Implications from Data

New Product Development

- Our speed to market of new products is key
- Cost reduction efforts for existing products
- Need to address product quality issues
- Threat of plastics taking share from our material
- New value-added products to satisfy needs of multi media market segment
- Need for different product offering for international markets

Supply Chain

- Partner with customers throughout the supply chain
- Develop web tools to support efficient supply chain processes such as order status, order entry, invoice status, tally sheets
- Reduce lead time and increase speed through supply chain
- Offer programs such as VMI, JIT
- Product availability to target customers throughout all market conditions

Service Offerings

- Improve on-time delivery. Target: 95%
- Knowledgeable, decision-making empowered sales and support groups that can be reached and solve customer issues quickly

Marketing Tools and Communication

- Programs to address the perception gap between prospects and current customers about us
- Continue to improve new product launches by focusing on flawless execution
- Need better handle on competitive intelligence through benchmarking of our products against competition to develop data based selling tools
- Leverage access and communication with customers to get a better handle on customer needs
- Need better understanding of import/export trends

Sales Effectiveness

- Develop data based selling programs
- Develop clearer, more executable sales strategies linked to Marketing Plans
- Work more closely with sales on translating marketing strategies into customer specific value propositions
- Help improve sales force product knowledge

Key Issues To Be Addressed By The Marketing Plan: Next Year
- Address threat of plastic taking share from our material
- Continue product innovation directed at high-end markets to create barriers for competition
- Address cost reduction efforts for existing products
- Address product and service issues to specific needs of international markets including stiffness, shade, brightness and yield
- Improve product performance
- Identify target customers and prospects for each segment and develop value propositions
- Continue to leverage premium pricing strategy
- Increase competitive intelligence and leverage lower customer total cost in use of our products
- Marketing communication plan to strengthen our position with customers and improve our perception with prospects addressing the gaps from customer satisfaction survey
- Work with sales to translate marketing strategies into actionable sales plans

Key Issues To Be Addressed By The Marketing Plan: Future Years
- Develop strategies for new business through select group of customers in target markets
- Develop web tools to support efficient supply chain processes such as order status, order entry, invoice status, tally sheets
- Work with sales to gain more customer intimacy

Key Issues Not Addressed By The Marketing Plan
- Need to address strategic issue of securing external business versus supplying internal divisions (to be addressed by Corporate Strategic Plan).
- Need to quickly diagnose customer technical problems and offer solutions (to be addressed by Technical Service Team).
- Customer service representatives need to respond quickly to customer needs (to be addressed by Service Team).

Objectives To Be Achieved By Segment: Marketing, Sales, Financial					
	Pharma	**Manufc.**	**Food**	**Multi Media**	**Global**
Current sales (units)	6.51	7.35	9.0	---	2.0
Current sales ($ million)	$327	$506	$117	---	$87
Next year target (units)	7.0	7.0	11.0	3.0	5.0
Next year target ($ million)	$330	$506	$130	$150	$225
Current market share	25%	43%	10%	---	5%
Target market share	25%	43%	15%	6%	11%
Current customer mix (%)	Premium: 25 Performance: 33 Value: 42	Premium: 10 Performance: 45 Value: 45	Premium: 5 Performance: 50 Value: 45	---	Global market segmentation not yet done
Target customer mix (%)	Premium: 30 Performance: 40 Value: 30	Premium: 15 Performance: 45 Value: 40	Premium: 15 Performance: 50 Value: 35	Premium: 45 Performance: 25 Value: 30	Global market segmentation not yet done
Current EBIT ($ million)	$70	$60	$85	---	$15
Target EBIT ($ million)	$80	$65	$100	$20	$30
Current product mix (million units)	ABC: 1.6 KLM: 3.2 XYZ: --- DEF: 0.25 GHI: 1.46	ABC: 2.5 KLM: 0.6 XYZ: 1.3 DEF: 0.95 GHI: 2.0	ABC: --- KLM: 1.7 XYZ: 2.2 DEF: --- GHI: 5.1	---	We only sell the ABC line in global markets
Target product mix (million units)	ABC: 2.0 KLM: 3.0 XYZ: --- DEF: 0.1 GHI: 1.9	ABC: 3.0 KLM: 1.0 XYZ: 1.0 DEF: 0.7 GHI: 1.3	ABC: 1.2 KLM: 2.0 XYZ: 3.0 DEF: --- GHI: 4.8	ABC: 1.0 KLM: 0.1 XYZ: 0.5 DEF: --- GHI: 1.4	Continue selling ABC line

OBJECTIVES TO BE ACHIEVED BY SEGMENT: MARKETING MIX					
	Pharma	**Manufc.**	**Food**	**Multi Media**	**Global**
Product objectives	Continue supporting this segment with current products. Introduce 2 new products to capture direct to consumer markets	Continue supporting this segment with current products	Introduce ABC line in this market segment. Develop 3 new products to capture emerging fast-casual market	Introduce all our product lines (except DEF) to this segment. Develop 2 new products to capture crossover media markets	Stay the course with this segment
Pricing objectives	Maintain price premiums	Protect price premiums	Increase price margins by value-added pricing and reducing cost to serve	Serve high-end customer segment. Maintain price premiums	Continue targeting high-end of market
Channel objectives	Continue with current channel objectives of dealing with large customers	Develop relationships with end customers	Develop channels to sell ABC line in this segment	Develop relationships with major players. Penetrate executive suite	Develop relationships with agents
Marketing communications objectives	Maintain current communication strategy of premium-priced, high value-added supplier	Mitigate brand image problems due to machine resizing issues	Strengthen perception with current customers and grow brand awareness with prospects	Communicate our total solutions concept	Grow identity with regional markets
Marketing research objectives	Send follow up customer satisfaction survey to assess if customers have noticed changes in service	Develop in-depth understanding of customer needs by cross-functional team approach	Understand customer decision making to reduce cost to serve	Develop customer panel to leverage relationships and obtain customer needs understanding	We need to do research to segment customers in this market

MARKETING STRATEGIES AND TACTICS

Product Strategy
- Create value added products for pharma, food and multi media segments
- Improve product quality

Product Tactics	Timing	Person Responsibility	Cost/ Resources Required	Metric To Track	Impact of Strategy
Introduce 2 new pharma products	Q2	A. Anders	$55,000	Units and EBIT	$35 million in EBIT in 3 years
Introduce ABC line into Food market segment	Q3	P. Drake	• $100,000 • Work with Supply Chain to align distribution channels • Coordinate with Sales counterpart to develop Marketing and Sales materials for customers	• Units • Market share • EBIT	• $100 million in sales in 3 years • $20 million EBIT/yr in 3 years
Introduce 2 new multi media products	Q3	A. Anders	$75,000	Units and EBIT	$50 million in EBIT in 5 years
Improve product quality at Pinemountain facility	Q1	J. Ray	• $25,000 • Work with Production	• Litmus test score of 7.5 • Customer complaints	• Reduce customer turnover by 20% in 1 year • 10 new customers in 2 years

MARKETING STRATEGIES AND TACTICS (continued)

Pricing Strategy

Continue to support premium pricing strategy by delivering superior value in goods and services to target markets and customers

Pricing Tactics	Timing	Person Responsibility	Cost/ Resources Required	Metric To Track	Impact of Strategy
Gain insight into customer needs and value drivers	Q1	J. Welk	• $40,000 • Deploy 4 cross-functional teams	Meeting segment objectives	Market share increase by 4.1%
Increase price margins in food segment	Q4	R. Draper	• Work with IT to develop on-line service mechanisms. • Total cost: $250,000	10% improvements in margins across the board next year	• Cost savings of $2 million over 3 years • $15 million EBIT improvement next year
Roll out sales tracking tools to all segments	Q3	J. Welk	• $150,000 • Work with Sales	% of product sold over industry average price	$7 EBIT improvement within 3 years

Channel Strategy
- Continue to build relationships with key end user customers
- Develop additional channels

Channel Tactics	Timing	Person Responsibility	Cost/ Resources Required	Metric To Track	Impact of Strategy
Develop relationships with key end use customers in manufacturing segment	Q2	C. Franks	• $30,000 • Coordinate with cross-functional members	# of direct relationships EBIT	EBIT improvement by $5 million next year
Penetrate executive suite in multi media segment	Q2	C. Franks	$10,000	5 new contracts secured next year	Sales impact: $30 million
Develop electronic channel for Pharma segment	Phase 1 by Q3	W. Burns	$250,000	1.2 million units next year	Sales impact: $13 million

MARKETING STRATEGIES AND TACTICS (continued)

Marketing Communications Strategy

Define corporate brand identity and communicate to target segments and customers

Tactics	Timing	Person Responsibility	Cost/ Resources Required	Metric To Track	Impact of Strategy
Print campaign to current customers to reinforce message about product quality and service levels	Q2	R. Brown	$85,000	Brand equity score increase to 8.9 (from current 7.5)	• Reduce customer turnover by 10% over 2 years
Develop sales materials to communicate Total Solutions concept	Q2	R. Brown	• $5,000 • Work with Sales to finalize material	Number of new customers	• Increase Premium customer mix to 30% next year
Other Tactics					
Follow up customer satisfaction survey	Q4	A. Circe	$5,000	Reduction in customer complaints by 25%	• Better customer relations • Process improve-ments in customer service

Positioning Relative to Competition

Our Marketing Plan will enable us to build a competitive advantage in the areas of penetrating Premium customers, premium price positioning, and strong product innovation.

	Product Strategy	Pricing Strategy	Channel Strategy	Marketing Communications Strategy
Us	• Marketing Plan enables us to demonstrate strong product innovation • Enables us to penetrate new markets	• Positions us squarely as a premium-priced, value-added player • Increases our Premium customer mix to 30%	• We have taken leadership role in industry with electronic channels	• This has traditionally been our weakest link • Marketing Plan strategies and tactics should see improvement in our brand image
Competitor A	Moves us beyond this competitor in product superiority	This competitor will emulate our strategy next year	Will provide us a competitive edge against this competitor for 2 years	• Strongest competitor • We will still lag behind this competitor in terms of brand image, but gap is narrowing
Competitor B	We have always been superior to this competitor. Gap should increase	Will most likely try to occupy a mid-market position	Will develop electronic channel capabilities, but without features in our offering	Our brand image is clearly superior to this competitor
Competitor C	Has never been known for product innovation	Will compete further on low prices	Will eventually be forced by customers to develop electronic channels	• Our brand image far superior to this competitor • We foresee this competitor exiting some markets we operate in

Marketing – Sales Linkage

Our business has excellent alignment from the Strategic Plan through the Marketing Plan to the Sales Plan as identified below.

Strategic Plan	Marketing Plan	Sales Plan
Develop new products and markets	• Introduce 2 new multimedia products • Introduce 2 new Pharma products • Introduce ABC line into Food market segment	• Target accounts: MediaGiant Inc., SMX Music, ABC Communications, Pioneer Symbols Inc. • Develop better customer relationships for product development initiatives • Establish customer value programs with Food market customers
Develop key strategic alliances	• Continue to build relationships with key end user segments • Develop additional channels	• Develop end user strategies with key customers (Acme, Belvedere, Tamaron, and Branson)
Reduce cost across the system	• Improve product quality at Pinemountain facility	• Initiate e-sales with key customers
Define and communicate corporate identity	• Print campaign to current customers to reinforce product quality message	• Develop Sales material to communicate Total Solutions Concept

Successful implementation of our Marketing Plan has implications for all functions:

- Marketing: Need to identify new product and market opportunities based on end consumer needs, as well as develop the Total Solutions Concept that will add value to our customers.
- Sales: Need to communicate our Total Solutions Concept to our customers, and incorporate our products and solutions into Customer Plans.
- Product Development: Need to continue to identify innovative products based on understanding of end consumer needs and trends to address the threat of plastic and other emerging materials.
- Supply Chain: Identify cost reduction opportunities from our suppliers to our customers by making entire process function in a more streamlined fashion. This not only adds value to our customers, but strengthens our competitive position as well.
- IT: Continue to support Sales in delivering additional value to our customers in a cost-effective fashion (e.g., e-sales). At the same time, find ways to integrate and use marketplace information available across functional groups.

Besides segment objectives outlined earlier, these are the value propositions we will offer our customers. The matrix below will be used by the Sales function to develop Key Account and Customer Plans.

	Premium	**Performance**	**Value**
Pharma	• Grade A product • Superior performance • Continuous availability • Dedicated Technical Service Team • No charge for special requests	• Product quality guarantees • High quality control standards • Aesthetic Widgets • Dedicated Technical Service Team	• Grade B product • Technical Team available as requested • Customer Service available as add-on
Manufc.	• Grade AA product • Superior performance • Inventory management • Dedicated Technical Service Team • No charge for special requests	• User friendly material • Quick turnaround • Lower Total Cost in Use guarantees	• Consistency in product • Sales materials • Guaranteed machine uptime
Food	• Grade A product • Custom Solutions Team • Dedicated Sales Team • No charge for special requests	• Cost containment guarantees • Security of supply • Product quality guarantees	• Diversified product line • Competitive price • Grade B product

TARGET CUSTOMER LIST					
Customer Segment	**Target Customer**	**Target Sales ($ million)**	**Pharma**	**Manufc.**	**Food**
Premium	Acme Co.	$10.4	✓		
	KLM Co.	$7.7		✓	
	Tamaron Ind.	$5.5	✓		✓
	DEF Co.	$4.5		✓	
	RST Co.	$3.9	✓	✓	
Performance	ABC Co.	$7.3	✓		✓
	Springhill Ltd.	$5.7	✓		

TARGET CUSTOMER LIST (continued)					
Customer Segment	Target Customer	Target Sales ($ million)	Pharma	Manufc.	Food
	AKS Inc.	$2.75		✓	
	CLT Co.	$1.34			✓
	Branson Ind.	$0.68		✓	
	Abby Intl.	$0.52	✓		
	Mack Bolts	$0.08	✓		
Value	PON Inc.	$2.2		✓	
	Reed Ind.	$1.4	✓		✓
	Flower Co.	$0.56			✓
	TSR Co.	$0.45	✓		
	Anson Ltd.	$4.1		✓	

Key Outcomes for the Business

If we execute our Marketing and Sales Plans flawlessly, key expected outcomes next year are:

	This Year	Next Year
Marketing Plan budget ($ million)	$0.9	$1.08
Sales (million units)	22.86	32
Sales ($ million)	$950	$1,340
EBIT ($ million)	$200	$295
Market share	30%	34.1
ROI	15%	17%

Marketing Plan Budget

Please see Key Marketing Strategies

Marketing Plan Control

- Each strategy has a set of tactics associated with it.
- Each tactic (action item) has a person responsible for completion, timelines, costs, and resources required
- For each tactic, goals are established by period (example shown below) to act as milestones
- Each month, the Marketing Director will receive a progress report on tactics from each individual
- Marketing and Sales, during their quarterly meetings (or more often, as necessary) will discuss Marketing and Sales program execution and make changes as necessary

Product Strategy: New Market Penetration
Tactic: Introduce ABC line into Food segment
Person Responsible: P. Drake

	Year 1 Goal	Year 2 Goal	Year 3 Goal	Comments
Sales (million units)	1.2	2.3	3.1	
Sales ($ million)	$20	$30	$50	
EBIT ($ million)	($0.25)	$5	$25	
Market share	1%	1.9%	3%	
Resources required	• Work with Supply Chain • Coordinate with Sales			• Well on track to achieve launch date of Q3. • Exploring factory direct route with Supply Chain. • Will work with Sales Q1 to develop customer materials.

Marketing Plan Appendix
Competitor A profile[31]

Meta merger afforded our top competitor a more complete product portfolio and stronger value proposition.

Opportunities
- Merge with another widget company overseas to increase presence internationally and acquire MN multi task manufacturing capacity
- Define better distribution strategy

Threats
- Substitute materials, ie plastics
- Customers' trend for material reduction
- Exchange rate disadvantages
- Growing material costs

Strengths
- Global supplier, strong international presence
- Focus and commitment to high-end markets
- Strong relationship with key customers
- Enhanced capabilities with merger
- Clear integration strategy

Weaknesses
- US production only
- Manufacturing disadvantage internationally
- Confusion on distributor strategy due to BXT acquisition
- Distracted by integration efforts, product quality issues

Leverage Points for Competitor vs. us
- European plants in key high end markets that use LDB technology
- Innovative new products in Pharma category
- Less constraint in Dura widget capacity
- More advanced in customer facing systems

Leverage Points for us
- Focus on technology (HDC)
- Offshore experience, especially in Asia with manufacturing
- Cross-functional value creation capabilities
- Joint venture structure, legal, cultural, etc.

Position by Segment	Tons	Sales	Share
Pharma	575	$403	24%
Food	300	$240	30%
Manufacturing	10	$12	15%
Multimedia	1,000	$800	35%

---

[31] I have only provided one competitor profile for illustration purposes.

Marketing Plan Appendix (continued)
Competitor A profile

What Actions Should We Take Against This Competitor?	**Sustainable Competitive Advantage for us**
• Leverage our offshore manufacturing experience to gain entry into Europe • Leverage our cross-functional expertise to solve customer problems • Continue to segment markets and customers	• Offshore manufacturing experience in Asia • Joint venture structure, legal, cultural, etc. • Resources to solve customer problems • Consistency of product performance

Appendix 2

Sales Plan Example[32]

Executive Summary
There are several key Sales issues we must address next year:

- ➢ Continue to leverage premium pricing strategy by lowering customer total cost in use and helping our customers penetrate new markets
- ➢ We need to improve our product quality and communicate to customers
- ➢ Significant new product development opportunities exist in Pharma and Food
- ➢ Opportunity to sell ABC line in Food market segment
- ➢ Opportunity exists to communicate Total Solutions Concept with customers
- ➢ Develop end user strategies with key customers
- ➢ E-selling opportunities with key customers

We have established the following Sales objectives for next year:

- ➢ Achieve $1.34 billion sales and $295 million EBIT through sales of 32,000,000 units, and increase market share by 4.1% next year
- ➢ Introduce 7 new products contributing $155 million sales and $30 million EBIT
- ➢ Strengthen our position with customers and improve our perception with prospects by improving top box ratings of customer satisfaction survey by 15%
- ➢ Grow international business to receive 5% share and 1,250,000 units resulting in sales of $140 million and generating $28 million EBIT
- ➢ Translate Marketing strategies into actionable Sales Plans by developing more compelling value propositions to our customers, resulting in an increase of Premium customers by 30%

In order to achieve our objectives we must focus on these key sales initiatives:
Financial

- ➢ Achieve sales targets of 33 m units, $1.341 bn sales, and $295 m EBIT

---

[32] As with the Marketing Plan, please do not attempt to do arithmetic computations to ensure my figures match. Numbers are for illustration purposes only.

Customers
- Introduce ABC line into Food market segment
- Introduce 2 new multi media products
- Reduce customer turnover by 10% next year
- Achieve target customer mix
- Follow up customer satisfaction survey
- Gain insight into customer needs and value drivers
- Develop relationships with key end use customers in manufacturing segment
- Penetrate executive suite in multi media segment
- Develop sales materials to communicate Total Solutions concept

Operations
- Reduce supply chain costs
- Roll out sales tracking tools to all segments

People
- Career development plans for sales force
- Improve sales product knowledge
- Attend 3 trade shows
- Develop sales consultative selling skills
- Hold 4 sales meetings

To successfully achieve our Sales objectives, we must work closely with Marketing to translate Marketing Plans into Sales and Key Account Plans. Further, successful implementation of initiatives will require us to work closely with other functions and coordinate programs. To achieve our objectives, we are budgeting $975,000 next year.

WIDGET BUSINESS OVERVIEW					
Product Line	Current Year Sales ($Million)	Market Share	5-Yr. Average ROI	5-Yr. Average EBIT ($ Million)	Current Year Capital Employed ($Million)
ABC	$350	15%	22%	$85	$100
KLM	$110	32%	15%	$37	$50
XYZ	$185	10%	7%	$26	$55
DEF	$55	5%	4%	$7	$72
GHI	$250	40%	17%	$45	$173
Total	**$950**	**30%**	**15.2%**	**$200**	**$450**

Our DEF product line continues to under perform, based on minimum ROI expectations of 7%.

Marketplace Analysis

Global expansion as well as large Manufacturers, Mass Merchants and Home Centers will play a key role in our strategies

Summary of Key Facts
- Global Widget market is 150 billion units with projected 4% annual market growth
- Increased pressure from alternative products such as plastics
- Internationally there are different product requirements
- Capacity growth in Asia, especially in BXC
- Higher visual appeal packaging requirements
- Supplier consolidation by customers
- Fewer and bigger customers
- Dominant retailers exert more control over our customers

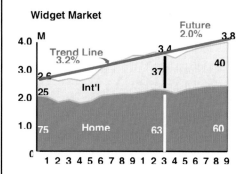

Widget Market

Source: Business Trends.

Implications of Key Facts
- Limited alternative manufacturing capabilities lessen our ability to grow share globally
- Consolidation through the entire value chain is driving the need for us to reduce total cost of products and services
- Current product offering limits our ability to compete globally due to stiffness, yield, and needs to be addressed
- New strategy in Europe needs to be implemented
- Due to major retailer dominance, effective merchandising will continue to be a critical component of product pull, thus requiring better, more technologically advanced packaging
- Need to analyze internal systems and measurements to better address product quality issues

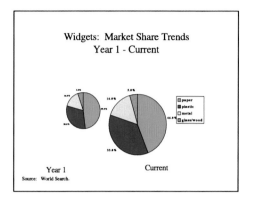

Widgets: Market Share Trends
Year 1 - Current

Year 1   Current
Source: World Search.

Channel of Distribution Trends
Key Facts:
- Channel dynamics continue to change as customers explore different channel options in an effort to become more efficient.
- Distributors are fighting to keep share and struggling to justify the true value that they offer in the supply chain.
- Printers are signing long-term supply agreements with key customers. Also, their contracts have punitive damage for material supplied by other distribution channels.
- Increasingly, large volume customers want a direct relationship with manufacturers.
- Distributor margins and receivables are under tremendous pressure.
- Customer-driven relationships facilitate solution selling and enable the creation of switching barriers.

Implications:
- In addition to providing value directly to end users, we must partner with major channel members to protect our share.
- We must make financial stability a key focus for next year.

Pricing Trends

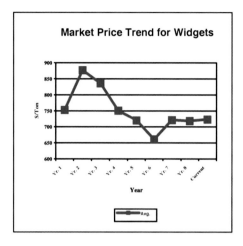

Market Price Trend for Widgets

Key Observations
- From Year 1 through current year pricing has gained ground from the lowest levels
- Pricing trend appears to be stabilizing at $700/unit
- We foresee this trend to continue

Implications
- Customer segmentation that began 2 years ago contributed to our ability to hold pricing
- Downtime, plant closings and other measures were taken to manage our capacity versus demand
- Strategy going forward should focus on eliminating downtime and maximizing profit by concentrating on most appropriate product and customer mix while leveraging value to support premium pricing

Marketplace Analysis: Summary of Business Implications

➢ Address threat of plastic taking share from away from us
  ➢ Develop widget materials to better compete with plastics
  ➢ Promote our material as a renewable, more environmental alternative
➢ Stronger focus on innovation
  ➢ Superior printability material and other value-add liners for higher impact packaging
➢ Need for different product offering for international markets
  ➢ Yield, stiffness, shade, brightness, etc.
➢ Continue customer segmentation and offer stronger value propositions to strengthen relationships with target customers
  ➢ We should focus on the right customer and product mix
➢ Need optimized selling and manufacturing strategy in international markets
  ➢ Production in Asia and Europe
  ➢ Value propositions for select customers
  ➢ Stronger relationships with agents
➢ We need to better manage capacity versus demand
  ➢ We need to think of forming a supply – demand allocation function
➢ Need to address global market dynamics as product and packaging move to low cost regions
  ➢ Better competitive intelligence
➢ Improve supply chain efficiencies through programs such as VMI, JIT, Internet tracking and on-time delivery
➢ Need to analyze internal systems and measurements to better address customer product quality issues

COMPETITOR ENVIRONMENT		
Competitor[33]	**Competitor Offering and Strategy**	**Our Sales Strategy**
Viking Industries	• High quality product • Full product line • Complete service offering • Aggressive pricing	• Do not compete on price • Sell Total Solution concept • Grow Premium customer business by 20%
Galt Inc.	• High quality product • Full product line • Limited sales coverage • Charges price premiums, but willing to negotiate	• Focus on our extensive sales coverage and support • Do not compete on price • Focus on Total Solutions concept
Bosworth	• Medium product quality, have had issues recently • Poor technical support • Potential strike situation threatens to disrupt operations	• Focus on our consistent supply capability • Target their customers • Grow Performance customer business by 30%
Grainger Mfc.	• Inconsistent product quality • Problems with raw material supply • Low priced competitor • Focus on low end of market	• Maintain share of Value customers • Focus on our improved product quality • Offer fixed package to customers

Segmentation Analysis: Markets and Customers

MARKET SEGMENT REVIEW: TRENDS					
	Pharma	**Manufc.**	**Food**	**Multi Media**	**Global**
Growth rate	7%	4%	10%	15%	22%
Pricing outlook (5 Yr.)	$150/unit	$120	$320	$175	$205
Our share	25%	43%	20%	0	5%
Profitability	Average	Average	Above avg.	Well above avg.	Well above avg.
Segment attractiveness	Average	Medium	High	High	High
Strategic fit	High	Medium	High	High	High
Segment decision	Maintain	Maintain	Grow	Grow	Grow

---

[33] For details on competitor SWOT analysis, refer to Marketing Plan

Multi media and global are new segments for us. As indicated above, our analysis reveals that they are very attractive segments and we must pursue them aggressively. Currently, we have not segmented the global market along the lines of our domestic market. This is a step that will be pursued in the future.

PRODUCT LINE SALES TO SEGMENTS								
Product Line	**Pharma (million units and $ million annual)**		**Manufc. (million units and $ million annual)**		**Food (million units and $ million annual)**		**Total**	
ABC	1.6	$150	2.5	$200	---	---	4.1	$350
KLM	3.2	$40	0.6	$40	1.7	$30	5.5	$110
XYZ	---	---	1.3	$140	2.2	$45	3.5	$185
DEF	0.25	$12	0.95	$43	---	---	1.2	$55
GHI	1.46	$125	2.0	$83	5.1	$42	8.56	$250

We currently do not offer our ABC line in the Food segment. Our analysis has revealed Food to be growing at 10% annually. Therefore, we should think about how we can secure channels of distribution for the ABC line in this segment.

The XYZ line is not offered currently in the Pharma market segment. However, our analysis indicates that we should not pursue this opportunity at the present time. Instead, resources should be devoted to penetrating the multi media segment, a growth opportunity for us.

The DEF product line is best represented in the manufacturing segment. Our decision with this segment is to maintain our presence. Currently, we serve the manufacturing segment with all of our product lines. Our analysis reveals that we should phase out the DEF line within the next 5 years.

PRODUCT LINE REVIEW					
Product Line	**Current Year Sales ($Million)**	**Market Share**	**5-Yr. Average ROI**	**5-Yr. Average EBIT ($ Million)**	**Current Year Capital Employed ($Million)**
ABC	$350	15%	22%	$85	$100
KLM	$110	32%	15%	$37	$50
XYZ	$185	10%	7%	$26	$55
DEF	$55	5%	4%	$7	$72
GHI	$250	40%	17%	$45	$173
Total	**$950**	**30%**	**15.2%**	**$200**	**$450**

Our DEF product line continues to under perform, based on minimum ROI expectations of 7%.

Customer Classification By Needs And Attractiveness

	Premium	Performance	Value
Pharma	• Highest-grade quality • Proactive technical support • Willing to pay price premiums	• Consistent product quality • System efficiencies • May consider price premiums if case is made	• Basic quality • Product bundling • Will not consider price premiums
Manufc.	• High-impact product • Proactive technical support • Willing to pay price premiums	• User friendly packages • Quick turnaround • May consider price premiums if case is made	• Consistency in product • Sales materials • Will not consider price premiums
Food	• Custom solutions • Security of supply • Willing to pay price premiums	• Cost containment • Security of supply • Will consider price premiums if case is made	• Diversified product line • Competitive price

CUSTOMER SEGMENT REVIEW					
Customer Segment	**Customer**	**Sales ($ million)**	**Cost to Serve ($/unit)**	**Customer Profitability ($/unit)**	**Decision**
Premium (total: 15 customers)	Belvedere Co. (Pharma)	$23	$12	$25	Grow
	Briar Co. (Food and Manufc.)	$42	$20	$15	Grow
	Cameron Co.	$100	$44	$4	Reduce cost to serve
	Deal Inc.	$15	$35	$17	Grow
	Real Co.	$5	$45	($20)	Negotiate contract for better terms or drop
Performance (total: 23 customers)	ABC Co.	$25	$25	$7	Shows signs of Value customer. Need further data to validate
	Bonyton Inc.	$11	$35	$12	Grow

CUSTOMER SEGMENT REVIEW (continued)					
Customer Segment	**Customer**	**Sales ($ million)**	**Cost to Serve ($/unit)**	**Customer Profitability ($/unit)**	**Decision**
	Bossier Ind.	$56	$26	$45	Potential to become Premium customer
	Catmatsu Co.	$78	$34	$23	Grow
Value (total: 30 customers)	Aim Co.	$34	$26	$17	Maintain
	Bruno Mfc.	$85	$11	$18	Maintain
	Caruthers Co.	$67	$15	$25	Potential to become Performance customer
	Eigen Mfc.	$12	$46	($15)	Reduce cost to serve or drop

Top Sales Issues and Opportunities
- We need to improve our product quality and communicate to customers
- Significant new product development opportunities exist in Pharma and Food
- Opportunity to sell ABC line in Food market segment
- Opportunity exists to communicate Total Solutions Concept with customers
- Develop end user strategies with key customers
- E-selling opportunities with key customers

TARGET CUSTOMER LIST					
Customer Segment	**Target Customer**	**Target Sales ($ million)**	**Pharma**	**Manufc.**	**Food**
Premium	Acme Co.	$10.4	✓		
	KLM Co.	$7.7		✓	
	Tamaron Ind.	$5.5	✓		✓
	DEF Co.	$4.5		✓	
	RST Co.	$3.9	✓	✓	
Performance	ABC Co.	$7.3	✓		✓
	Springhill Ltd.	$5.7	✓		
	AKS Inc.	$2.75		✓	
	CLT Co.	$1.34			✓
	Branson Ind.	$0.68		✓	
	Abby Intl.	$0.52	✓		
	Mack Bolts	$0.08	✓		
Value	PON Inc.	$2.2		✓	
	Reed Ind.	$1.4	✓		✓
	Flower Co.	$0.56			✓
	TSR Co.	$0.45	✓		
	Anson Ltd.	$4.1		✓	

TARGET PROSPECT LIST				
Target Prospect	**Sales Potential ($ million)**	**Pharma**	**Manufc.**	**Food**
Natal Co.	$25.1	✓		✓
Brunkal Ind.	$24.2		✓	
Hawk Ind.	$19.5	✓	✓	
Socrates Ltd.	$17.8	✓	✓	
Bosworth Co.	$16.4	✓		
Liverpool Co.	$16.2	✓		
Polanco Ltd.	$14.1	✓		
Roma Inc.	$12.5		✓	
Condesa Ltd.	$12.0			✓
KLT Ind.	$11.1		✓	
Angel Intl.	$10.7	✓		
MTC Bolts	$10.6	✓		
Bela Ind.	$8.4			✓
Tami Ind.	$7.2	✓		✓
Joy Co.	$5.2	✓		
AND Co.	$3.3		✓	
Leyden Ind.	$2.1	✓	✓	

PERFORMANCE TARGETS BY SEGMENT

	Pharma	Manufc.	Food	Multi Media	Global
Current sales (units)	6.51	7.35	9.0	---	2.0
Current sales ($ million)	$327	$506	$117	---	$87
Next year target (units)	7.0	7.0	11.0	3.0	5.0
Next year target ($ million)	$330	$506	$130	$150	$225
Current market share	25%	43%	10%	---	5%
Target market share	25%	43%	15%	6%	11%
Current customer mix (%)	Premium: 25 Performance: 33 Value: 42	Premium: 10 Performance: 45 Value: 45	Premium: 5 Performance: 50 Value: 45	---	Global market segmentation not yet done
Target customer mix (%)	Premium: 30 Performance: 40 Value: 30	Premium: 15 Performance: 45 Value: 40	Premium: 15 Performance: 50 Value: 35	Premium: 45 Performance: 25 Value: 30	Global market segmentation not yet done
Current EBIT ($ million)	$70	$60	$85	---	$15
Target EBIT ($ million)	$80	$65	$100	$20	$30
Current product mix (million units)	ABC: 1.6 KLM: 3.2 XYZ: --- DEF: 0.25 GHI: 1.46	ABC: 2.5 KLM: 0.6 XYZ: 1.3 DEF: 0.95 GHI: 2.0	ABC: --- KLM: 1.7 XYZ: 2.2 DEF: --- GHI: 5.1	---	We only sell the ABC line in global markets
Target product mix (million units)	ABC: 2.0 KLM: 3.0 XYZ: --- DEF: 0.1 GHI: 1.9	ABC: 3.0 KLM: 1.0 XYZ: 1.0 DEF: 0.7 GHI: 1.3	ABC: 1.2 KLM: 2.0 XYZ: 3.0 DEF: --- GHI: 4.8	ABC: 1.0 KLM: 0.1 XYZ: 0.5 DEF: --- GHI: 1.4	Continue selling ABC line

SALES PERFORMANCE TARGETS: ABC PRODUCT LINE[34]						
Customer Segment	**Customer**	**Market Segment**	**Current Year Sales (million units)**	**Current Year Sales ($ million)**	**Next Year Sales Target (million units)**	**Next Year Sales Target ($ million)**
Premium	Belvedere Co.	Pharma	0.055	$23	0.13	$25.875
	Briar Co.	Food Manufc.	1.1	$42	1.3	$45
	Cameron Co.	Pharma	2.3	$100	2.4	$100.3
	Deal Inc.	Food		ABC line currently not sold in Food		
	Real Co.	Pharma Food	0.006	$5	0.008	$6.4
	MM Inc.	Multi media	---	---	0.05	$2.2
Performance	ABC Co.	Manufc.	1.0	$25	1.0	$25
	Bonyton Inc.	Manufc.	0.5	$11	1.1	$25.2
	Bossier Ind.	Pharma	2.0	$56	2.5	$60.0
	Catmatsu Co.	Food		ABC line currently not sold in Food		
	Mars Media	Multi media	---	---	0.9	$2.3
Value	Aim Co.	Pharma	3.0	$34	3.0	$34
	Bruno Mfc.	Food		ABC line currently not sold in Food		
	Caruthers Co.	Food Manufc.	5.0	$67	7.5	$80.0
	Eigen Mfc.	Pharma	1.0	$12	0.5	$6
	Musicx Ltd.	Multi media	---	---	1.0	$13
	Pacific Ind.	Global	1.5	$20.0	1.7	$21.2
	Transglobal	Global	0.5	$9.0	0.6	$9.3
	Komaron Ind.	Global	Currently do not serve –	---	0.2	$5.0

---

[34] I have only included one product line for illustration purposes.

KEY SALES INITIATIVES					
Financial Initiatives	**Timing**	**Person Responsibility**	**Cost/ Resources Required**	**Metric To Track**	**Impact of Initiative**
Achieve sales targets of 33 m units, $1.341 bn sales, and $295 m EBIT	Year	Sales team	See initiatives below	Units, sales, EBIT	Meeting sales objectives
Customer Initiatives	**Timing**	**Person Responsibility**	**Cost/ Resources Required**	**Metric To Track**	**Impact of Initiative**
Introduce ABC line into Food market segment	Q3	B. Bela	• $100,000 • Work with Supply Chain to align distribution channels • Coordinate with Marketing to develop Marketing and Sales materials for customers	• Units • Market share • EBIT	• $100 million in sales in 3 years • $20 million EBIT/yr in 3 years
Introduce 2 new multi media products	Q3	A. Sims	$75,000	Units and EBIT	$50 million in EBIT in 5 years
Reduce customer turnover by 10% next year	Q4	A. Sims	Incorporated in other initiatives	Customer turnover	$20 million over 2 years
Achieve target customer mix	Q4	F. Chow	Incorporated in other initiatives	Achieving sales objectives	$65 million in EBIT in 3 years

KEY SALES INITIATIVES (continued)					
Customer Initiatives	**Timing**	**Person Responsibility**	**Cost/ Resources Required**	**Metric To Track**	**Impact of Initiative**
Follow up customer satisfaction survey	Q4	M. Granger	$5,000	Reduction in customer complaints by 25%	• Better customer relations • Process improvements in customer service
Gain insight into customer needs and value drivers	Q1	M. Granger	• $40,000 • Lead 4 cross-functional teams to customer sites	Meeting segment objectives	• Market share increase by 4.1%
Develop relationships with key end use customers in manufacturing segment	Q2	C. Fina	• $30,000 • Coordinate with cross-functional members	• # of direct relationships • EBIT	EBIT improvement by $5 million next year
Penetrate executive suite in multi media segment	Q2	C. Fina	$10,000	5 new contracts secured next year	Sales impact: $30 million
Develop sales materials to communicate Total Solutions concept	Q2	S. Ramirez	• $5,000 • Work with Marketing to finalize materials	Number of new customers	• Increase Premium customer mix to 30% next year
Operational Initiatives	**Timing**	**Person Responsibility**	**Cost/ Resources Required**	**Metric To Track**	**Impact of Initiative**
Reduce supply chain costs	Q2	M. Garcia	$100,000	Cost reduction	$900,000
Roll out sales tracking tools to all segments	Q3	P. Drummond	• $150,000 • Work with Marketing	% of product sold over industry average price	$7 million EBIT improvement within 3 years

KEY SALES INITIATIVES (continued)					
People Initiatives	Timing	Person Responsibility	Cost/ Resources Required	Metric To Track	Impact of Initiative
Career development plans for sales force	Q2	T. Tomkins	$20,000	Complete on time	Employee turnover reduction by 15%
Improve sales product knowledge	Q2	T. Tomkins	$50,000	Complete on time	Higher customer satisfaction scores
Attend 3 trade shows	Year	Team	$250,000	Complete as scheduled	Increase customer base by 20% in 3 years
Develop sales consultative selling skills	Q3	S. Ramirez	$100,000	Training scheduled for July	Higher customer retention metrics
Hold 4 sales meetings	Year	A. Sims	$40,000	Complete as scheduled	Better team work

DIRECTION FOR KEY ACCOUNT PREPARATION[35]			
Value Proposition	Premium Customer	Performance Customer	Value Customer
Marketing Support			
Industry trends	X		
End user needs and insights	X		
Manufacturing			
Consistent product quality	X	X	X
Custom orders	X		
Customer visits	X	X	X
Technical support	X	X	
Supply Chain			
Website for tracking orders	X	X	X
Vendor Managed Inventory	X		

---

[35] While provided for illustration purposes only, this is a pivotal table, as the sales function uses it to develop customer-specific value propositions.

CUSTOMER ACTION PLAN: BELVEDERE WIDGET INC.				
Initiative	**Key Steps**	**Responsibility**	**Timeline**	**Status**
Additional shipment of 75,000 units of ABC line	• Negotiate with customer procurement function • Finalize shipment arrangements with our supplier • Coordinate internal production issues	• A. Briar (Sales) • T. Wallen (Production)	• Q3 • Q3 • Q4	As of November of this year, we are in a strong position to accomplish this objective due to discussions that have taken place between us and customer
Customer paperwork reduction program	• Develop protocols for ordering, invoicing and payment	• B. Blain (Sales Admin) • A. Samuel (IT)	• Q1	We have experience with this program. Therefore, we anticipate no problem meeting the deadline
"Virtual Warehouse" service	• Agree on inventory levels • Coordinate supply chain activities	• C. Tomkins (Supply Chain)	• Q1 • Q3	As of November we have had some delays in inventory level agreements. We anticipate an agreement early next year

CUSTOMER ACTION PLAN: BELVEDERE WIDGET INC. (continued)				
Initiative	**Key Steps**	**Responsibility**	**Timeline**	**Status**
Home heating market penetration	• Conduct market research to assess consumer needs • Arrange initial meeting with supply chain partners to discuss raw material, production and shipment issues • Launch pilot in Northeast	• M. Gomes (Marketing) • B. Blain (Sales) • T. Wallen (Production)	• Q1 • Q2 • Q4	Secondary research has been completed and we (customer and us) are working actively to launch pilot Q4 next year

Belvedere Widget Inc.: Customer Action Plan Implementation and Budgets				
Initiative	**Success Metrics**	**Control**	**Competitive Response**	**Contingency Plan**
Additional shipment of 75,000 units of ABC line	• Target: 75,000 units • Q1: 5,000 • Q2: 15,000 • Q3: 25,000 • Q4: 30,000	Cross-functional team to meet every quarter to discuss progress. Sales and Production to send semi-monthly updates.	Competitor 2 is most likely to respond with a price cut.	Ensure communication with customer is high at all times
Customer paperwork reduction program	• Target: $150,000 in annual savings	No specific control mechanisms given the short deadline for this initiative. After implementation, Sales Admin and IT will track for 1 year	Competitive response likely in the form of attempts to create customer value in other areas	We must deploy our cross-functional teams more often to understand customer needs and value drivers
"Virtual Warehouse" service	• Target: $1.2 million • Q1: 0 • Q2: 0 • Q3: $50,000 • Q4: $300,000	Given the significant time required for ramping up this initiative, it will be monitored closely. Supply Chain to provide monthly updates at Leadership Team meetings.	We estimate this initiative to be difficult for our competitors to imitate easily. We think they will explore such opportunities with other customers	We must ensure that our customer completely understands the costs and benefits of this program.
Home heating market penetration	• Target: $12 million • Q1: 0 • Q2: 0 • Q3: 0 • Q4: $2.5 million	Marketing, Sales and Production to provide updates quarterly at cross-functional team meetings.	We have been very careful with this program in terms of market signaling. Competitor 3 is in best position to launch a similar program with Carson Industries	While we have been trying to get Carson's business, our efforts have not been successful so far. Our plan is to analyze Carson's market segmentation efforts to identify opportunities. We envision a partnership with Competitor 3 in the future to jointly serve Carson Industries

Appendix 3

Key Account (Customer) Plan Example

CUSTOMER DESCRIPTION	
Customer Name: Belvedere Widget Inc. **Address:** 2323 Bear Avenue Forest, CA 23232 **Employees:** 55,000 **Operations:** Operations in 50 countries; sales in 140 countries **Structure & Ownership:** Publicly traded corporation. **SIC CODE:** 2323 **Officers:** John Smith – Chairman & CEO Jill Jones – President	**Mission:** To improve living standards everywhere. **Company Values:** We value our employees, customers, suppliers and the communities were operate in. We are dedicated to running a profitable business while operating in the highest ethical standards. **Website:** www.belvederewidget.com **Brands:** Heavy widget, Light Widget, Flexo Widget, Dura Widget **Key Competitor:** Gizmo Corp.

CUSTOMER PERFORMANCE					
Product Line	**Total Shipments (Current Year)**	**Our Share**	**Competitor 1**	**Competitor 2**	**Other**
ABC	55,000	45%	15%	25%	15%
KLM	100,000	25%	25%	20%	30%
XYZ	45,000	55%	5%	15%	25%
DEF	75,000	-	-	45%	55%
GHI	25,000	-	20%	20%	60%
Totals	300,000	25%	15%	25%	35%

CUSTOMER PERFORMANCE (continued)					
Product Line	**Yr. 1 Shipments**	**Yr. 1 Goals**	**Yr. 2 Shipments**	**Yr. 2 Goals**	**Trends**
ABC	25,000	20,000	30,000	30,000	Positive
KLM	27,000	15,000	32,000	30,000	Positive
XYZ	5,000	8,000	4,500	9,000	Negative
DEF	10,000	10,000	15,000	15,000	Steady
GHI	2,000	1,500	3,000	2,500	Positive

We have not had any major claims against our products with this account. Last year, due to machine resizing efforts at our Bloomfield plant, we had some claims against the XYZ product line. However, these issues have now been fixed and we do not anticipate major claims next year.

During the last 5 years, our cross-functional teams have visited this account for a total of 10 times. On average, each visit lasted 2 days. During the same time period, this customer has visited us for a total of 6 times. Detailed trip reports may be obtained from our Sales & Marketing intranet.

CUSTOMER BUYING PROCESS					
Buying Criteria	**Importance To Customer**	**Our Rank**	**Competitor A**	**Competitor B**	**Competitor C**
Product mix	2	2	1	1	3
Product quality	1	2	1	2	4
Pricing	5	3	2	1	2
Technical service	5	1	2	2	3
Supply chain	4	1	1	2	1
Strategic fit	1	1	2	3	3

CUSTOMER BUYING PROCESS (continued)	
Buying Criteria	**Comments**
Product mix	Our customer has been urging us to diversify our product lines, we are currently seen as lagging behind our major competitors by a small margin.
Product quality	We have done well on this criterion with our customer in the past. However, our rank has slipped recently because of our machine resizing problems at Bloomfield.
Pricing	Our customer has ranked us behind our competitors on this dimension. However, two issues are paramount: they are willing to consider non-price variables in their decision-making equation and, they recognize our strengths in terms of strategic fit and product quality.
Technical service	We create value for this customer by providing excellent technical service as part of our product offering.
Supply chain	We rank higher on this criterion compared to our competitors. Investments made by us in supply chain improvements 3 years ago are starting to pay off.
Strategic fit	Perhaps our biggest competitive advantage, we offer this customer access to goods and services globally.
Buying Center	Our prime contact at this customer is Sally Smith, the purchasing agent. Other key influencers are John James (engineering), Molly Madsen (finance) and Ted Timmins (sales). Together, these individuals comprise the buying center. Our sales force has, over time, made inroads into building relationships with members of the buying center other than the purchasing agent. This strategy is going well. Further, we are actively engaged in penetrating the C-Suite: CEO (Chief Executive Officer), COO (Chief Operating Officer) and CMO (Chief Marketing Officer). This will solidify our relationship with this customer in the coming months.

CUSTOMER NEEDS ANALYSIS
Strategic Direction Being Pursued By Customer: Our customer wants to be known in their marketplace as a total solutions provider to their customers. Traditionally, this industry has been rather conservative, but our customer is very innovative in their strategies. They not only want to offer the basics (product quality, on-time deliveries, etc.) to their customers, but they are actively looking to build superior value for their customers. This customer's strategy fits perfectly with our own business philosophy. We can help them in their quest to become a total solutions provider by looking after their inventory, providing marketing research insights into their value chain and helping them offer differentiated products to their customers.

CUSTOMER NEEDS ANALYSIS (continued)

Customer Business Priorities For Next Year:
- Increase market share by 3%.
- Increase top-line growth by 5%.
- Increase profitability by 6%.
- Take out $25 million dollars in costs by consolidating operations.
- Introduce 3 new products.

How Does Our Customer Compete?

Our customer competes by creating value for their customers. They do so primarily by exploiting the value chain by understanding the needs of their customer's customer. Further, they are building relationships with the end customer in addition to selling their goods through traditional channels of distribution. Next year, they will launch a new e-business venture to supply the needs of customers located in rural areas more efficiently.

How Can We Help Our Customer Reduce Costs?

We have broken down our customer's costs into four areas:

Acquire: We have an opportunity to decrease our customer's acquisition costs by reducing their paperwork load. We estimate that this will generate $250,000 in annual cost savings.

Possess: By launching our new "virtual warehouse" service, we have significantly reduced our customer's inventory possession costs. However, opportunities still exist to help them reconfigure their warehouses for optimum product handling. This should generate an additional $3 million in cost savings annually.

Use: Our cross-functional teams visit this customer at least twice yearly. During these visits, they examine our customer's assembly operations to recalibrate, simplify and reduce wastage. Last year, for example, we found a significant error in machine #1 in our customer's Springhill location. Our cross-functional team was successful in correcting the problem and, in the process, increasing our customer's product quality quotient by 4%.

Dispose: Significant opportunities exist to help our customer with their recycling efforts. We need to examine the possibility of taking over this function and reduce their costs. Opportunities for either price increases or higher volume need to be examined.

CUSTOMER SWOT ANALYSIS[36]

Opportunities[37]:
- Launch existing products in home heating market. This is a new market for this customer and will mean a bold move by a competitor in this industry.
- Opportunity to increase market share in current market being served.
- Solidify position as total solutions provider.
- Opportunity to serve the mid-market segment.

Threats:
- Competitor 1 is launching a new product based on generation 2b3 technology.
- Lower priced widgets from abroad could erode market share.
- Raw material prices expected to rise sharply next year.

Strengths:
- Strong product mix and quality perceptions in the marketplace.
- Ability to build relationships with end customer.
- Dynamic, entrepreneurial management team.
- Fast, decision making culture.

Weaknesses:
- High cost of operations compared to competitors.
- Do not have the capabilities to serve the mid-market segment.
- Do not have the expertise to penetrate the home-heating segment.

How Can We Help This Customer?
- Our engineering group has the capability to help our customer develop the expertise to penetrate the home heating market.
- We have to help our customer further simplify their operations and reduce their costs.
- Our Marketing group can work with customer to develop a plan to serve the needs of the mid-market segment.
- By partnering even more, we can help this customer position themselves as a total solutions provider. To do this, we have to develop joint business plans.

---

[36] Remember, even though I am labeling this section a SWOT analysis, in reality it is an OTSW analysis, as we discussed in Chapter 4 on how to use the Marketing Plan template.

[37] These are opportunities and threats faced by our customers, and strengths and weaknesses they possess to exploit opportunities or mitigate threats.

KEY ACCOUNT ANALYSIS

Customer Marketplace Performance and Financial Health

Brand	Last Year Revenues	5 – Year Trend	Profit Margin	5-Yr. Trend
Heavy Widget	$2.5 billion	+ 7%	19.5%	+ 5%
Light Widget	$4.3 billion	+ 15%	16.2%	+ 11%
Flexo Widget	$1.7 billion	+ 10%	10.5%	+ 15%
Dura Widget	$0.5 billion	NA	9.2%	NA

Belvedere Widget Inc. has a strong record in the marketplace. Their revenues have been increasing steadily the last 5 years, with a corresponding increase in profit margins. Their latest line, Dura Widget, is off to a slow start, but we feel once the channel of distribution glitches are worked out, this will be a high-performing brand for our customer. Belvedere Widget has always paid their invoices on time, within the specifications of our SLA with them. They are in excellent financial shape, with cash reserves of $2.5 billion.

Current and Historical Relationships With Our Company

Due to machine resizing efforts at our Bloomfield plant, we had some claims against our XYZ product line. This caused product recall issues for our customer and created tension between our two organizations. In response, our CEO met with Belvedere's CEO and we have put in place joint programs to avoid such problems in the future.

Historically, our relationships with this customer have been excellent. Even the transition from a pure purchasing focus to penetration of the buying center has proceeded with minimal problems.

How Important Is This Customer To Us? Do They Fit Our Segmentation and Value Proposition Strategy?

Belvedere Widget Inc. is a strategic account. We anticipate that, over the next few years, we will grow strategically with this customer as our programs become even more entwined. From a strategy perspective, this customer is crucial to our marketplace strategy of providing turnkey solutions to our customers.

Our Strategic Plan calls for us to make a significant push into the widget market over the next five years. Belvedere Widget Inc. is a major player in this market and, therefore, a significant potential partner for us.

KEY ACCOUNT ANALYSIS (continued)				
How Does Customer View Suppliers? Is There Compatibility Between Us?				
Belvedere Widget Inc. is aware of the need for supplier development in order to achieve their marketplace goals. Therefore, they carefully select suppliers and grow with a reduced set of suppliers. Over time, their strategy has been to consolidate their supplier base. We expect this trend to continue. There is significant compatibility between us and the customer. Our compatibility has improved after we started bridging relationships between the two executive offices.				

Quantification of Customer Opportunities

Opportunity	Benefit To Customer	Economic Value To Customer (Annual)	Benefit To Us	Economic Value To Us (Annual)
Additional shipment of 75,000 units of ABC line	Helps customer increase shipments of Dura Widget line	We estimate this at additional $70 million	Helps us ship more of our most profitable product line	$32 million
Customer paperwork reduction program	Savings on resources that can be allocated elsewhere	$250, 000	Helps us simplify our business operations with customer.	$150,000
"Virtual Warehouse" service	Reduces customer's inventory costs	$3 million	Smoothes our production forecasting	$1.2 million
Help customer penetrate home heating market	New market opportunity for our customer	$35 million annual revenue potential	Enables us to ship more of our GHI product line	$12 million in additional sales

KEY ACCOUNT ANALYSIS (continued)				
Current Profit Level With Customer	**Profit Potential Within Next 1 Year**	**What Do We Need to do To Capitalize On Opportunities?**	**What Is Our Cost to Create Customer Value?**	**What is Our Return?**
Currently, our profit level with this customer is at $54 million	We believe, based on the programs we want to put in place, our profit level with this customer can be $99 million	• Need to negotiate a contract to ship additional units of ABC line • We are already underway to put in place the "virtual warehouse" concept. Our technical department has to meet in Q1 with their procurement function • Our Marketing function is already working with customer to develop joint program to penetrate home heating market	We estimate our total cost to create customer value at $15 million	Our return from investment is estimated at 24%

Decision Regarding Customer?
Clearly, Belvedere Widget Inc. is a strategic customer we want to grow with. We anticipate the opportunity for joint work and market penetration to grow in the next 3–5 years with this customer.

KEY ACCOUNT SALES PLAN						
Product Line	Next Year Shipments (Budget)	$/Unit	Standard Cost	Freight	Other Costs	Profit/Unit
ABC	130,000	$345	$110	$40	-	$195
KLM	100,000	$120	$70	$26	$8	$16
XYZ	60,000	$94	$75	-	$4	$15
DEF	80,000	$85	$35	$14	$10	$26
GHI	45,000	$240	$125	$25	-	$90

Initiative	Key Steps	Responsibility	Timeline	Status
Additional shipment of 75,000 units of ABC line	• Negotiate with customer procurement function • Finalize shipment arrangements with our supplier • Coordinate internal production issues	• A. Briar (Sales) • T. Wallen (Production)	• Q3 • Q3 • Q4	As of November of this year, we are in a strong position to accomplish this objective due to discussions that have taken place between us and customer
Customer paperwork reduction program	• Develop protocols for ordering, invoicing and payment	• B. Blain (Sales Admin) • A. Samuel (IT)	• Q1	We have experience with this program. Therefore, we anticipate no problem meeting the deadline
"Virtual Warehouse" service	• Agree on inventory levels • Coordinate supply chain activities	• C. Tomkins (Supply Chain)	• Q1 • Q3	As of November we have had some delays in inventory level agreements. We anticipate an agreement early next year

KEY ACCOUNT SALES PLAN (continued)				
Initiative	**Key Steps**	**Responsibility**	**Timeline**	**Status**
Home heating market penetration	• Conduct market research to assess consumer needs	• M. Gomes (Marketing) • B. Blain (Sales) • T. Wallen (Production)	• Q1	Secondary research has been completed and we (customer and us) are working actively to launch pilot Q4 next year
	• Arrange initial meeting with supply chain partners to discuss raw material, production and shipment issues		• Q2	
	• Launch pilot in Northeast		• Q4	

KEY ACCOUNT SALES PLAN CONTROL				
Initiative	**Success Metrics**	**Control**	**Competitive Response**	**Contingency Plan**
Additional shipment of 75,000 units of ABC line	• Target: 75,000 units • Q1: 5,000 • Q2: 15,000 • Q3: 25,000 • Q4: 30,000	Cross-functional team to meet every quarter to discuss progress. Sales and Production to send semi-monthly updates.	Competitor 2 is most likely to respond with a price cut.	Ensure communication with customer is high at all times
Customer paperwork reduction program	• Target: $150,000 in annual savings	No specific control mechanisms given the short deadline for this initiative. After implementation, Sales Admin and IT will track for 1 year	Competitive response likely in the form of attempts to create customer value in other areas	We must deploy our cross-functional teams more often to understand customer needs and value drivers

151

KEY ACCOUNT SALES PLAN CONTROL (continued)				
Initiative	**Success Metrics**	**Control**	**Competitive Response**	**Contingency Plan**
"Virtual Warehouse" service	• Target: $1.2 million • Q1: 0 • Q2: 0 • Q3: $50,000 • Q4: $300,000	Given the significant time required for ramping up this initiative, it will be monitored closely. Supply Chain to provide monthly updates at Leadership Team meetings.	We estimate this initiative to be difficult for our competitors to imitate easily. We think they will explore such opportunities with other customers	We must ensure that our customer completely understands the costs and benefits of this program.
Home heating market penetration	• Target: $12 million • Q1: 0 • Q2: 0 • Q3: 0 • Q4: $2.5 million	Marketing, Sales and Production to provide updates quarterly at cross-functional team meetings.	We have been very careful with this program in terms of market signaling. Competitor 3 is in best position to launch a similar program with Carson Industries	While we have been trying to get Carson's business, our efforts have not been successful so far. Our plan is to analyze Carson's market segmentation efforts to identify opportunities. We envision a partnership with Competitor 3 in the future to jointly serve Carson Industries

Glossary

Competitive Analysis
An analysis of our competitors to see what they are doing to take business away from us and, therefore, what we should be doing to become better competitors. Chapters 3, 4 and Appendix 1.

Cross-functional Team
A team comprising of representatives from different functions within a business – Marketing, Sales, Production, Human Resources, Finance, Accounting, IT, Supply Chain, Customer Service, etc. that makes joint decisions about understanding-creating-delivering-managing customer value. Chapter 7.

JIT
Just In Time. A supplier initiative, JIT programs deliver goods to the customer's location on a just in time basis so the customer's inventory carrying costs are minimized.

Key Account (Customer) Plan
A Key Account Plan is developed for key customer. It has two parts: a customer profile (that enables us to make a decision regarding this customer) and a sales plan for the customer (objectives to be achieved, sales tactics, etc.). Chapter 6 provides a template for developing a Key Account Plan and Appendix 3 provides an example of such a plan.

Key Issues
A set of issues the business plans to address next year with its Marketing, Sales and Key Account (Customer) Plans. A key issue is a key fact that has been synthesized. Here is an example. Key fact: "We face low priced competitors in the widget market." Key issue: "Low priced competitors in the widget market compel us to examine our market segmentation strategy to focus on higher-margin customers." Chapters 3, 4 and Appendix 1.

Key Performance Measures (KPM)
Also called Key Performance Indicators (KPI). Key Performance Measures refer to a set of metrics a business might put in place to measure how well it is doing in the marketplace. Many businesses use the concept of Scorecards to measure performance. For example, a typical Scorecard may contain four measures: profits, customers, processes, people.

Macroenvironmental Factors
These are such factors as economic, social, political, regulatory, cultural and demographic that will impact a business. Chapters 3, 4.

Market Segmentation
The concept of market segmentation says that different customers have different needs and these needs are constantly changing. Therefore, a business has two strategic questions it must ask – what needs (segments) are we going to serve and how? The first is called selecting the target market. The second is called positioning our offering in the marketplace. Chapter 2 provides a primer on market segmentation.

Marketing
A business function whose role (with the Sales function) is to understand – create – deliver – manage customer value.

Marketing Mix
Marketing Mix refers to a firm's product strategy, pricing strategy, channel of distribution strategy and marketing communications strategy. Chapters 3, 4, and Appendix 1.

Marketing Plan
A one-year slice of the Strategic Plan, the Marketing Plan first analyzes the external environment (customers, competitors, markets) facing the business. Coupled with internal strengths and weaknesses, the Marketing Plan then outlines some key issues the business must address during the coming year. Strategies, tactics to address the key issues are detailed and the Marketing Plan ends with a control section that acts like a rudder on a ship to ensure the Marketing Plan is a living, breathing document. Chapters, 3, 4, 5 discuss Marketing Plan development. Appendix 1 contains an example of a Marketing Plan.

Operating Plan

The collection of Marketing and other functional plans (Sales, Manufacturing, HR, IT, etc.) that provides specifics on the firm's operations for the upcoming year. Typically, an Operating Plan will include objectives to be achieved and budgets to achieve those objectives.

Performance Measurement

Typically, a business will put in place a set of measures (metrics) to see how well it is doing. These include financial measures such as profitability, customer measures such as satisfaction, operational measures such as capacity utilization, people measures such as employee satisfaction, etc. Chapter 3.

Sales

A business function whose role (with the Marketing function) is to understand – create – deliver – manage customer value.

Sales Plan

Also called a Sales Operating Plan, this plan provides direction for the development of Key Account (Customer) Plans. Sales Plans are developed depending upon how the business deploys its sales force – by geography, segment or a hybrid approach. Chapter 6 outlines a Sales Plan template while Appendix 2 provides an example.

Strategic Plan

The highest level plan developed in any business, it looks mountain top to mountain top to specify the medium to long term future of the company. In many companies, it is developed for a period of 3 –5 years and is updated yearly. Chapter 3 provides details.

Supply Chain

Interconnections between suppliers and customers used to get greater efficiencies in buying, making, moving and selling materials and goods. Chapter 3, Appendices 1 and 3.

SWOT Analysis

An analysis of the Opportunities, Threats, Strengths and Weaknesses facing a business to distill key issues that must be addressed by the business next year. Opportunities and Threats are typically external, while Strengths and Weaknesses are internal to the business. Chapters 3, 4 and Appendices 1 and 3.

Tactics

Actions taken to implement strategies. For example, our marketing communication strategy could be to develop awareness of our brand. A tactic could be to attend trade shows to boost awareness levels. Chapters 3, 4, 6 and Appendices 1, 2, 3.

Value Chain Analysis

A technique used to create value for our customers without having to ask them what their needs are. Chapter 4 provides an example.

Value Proposition

Developed at two levels, segment and customer, value propositions specify the offering (in terms of goods, services, relationships, information, etc.) we plan to develop for the marketplace. Chapter 2, and Appendices 1, 2, 3 provide examples.

Vendor Managed Inventory (VMI)

A program wherein the vendor (supplier) automatically manages inventory on behalf of the customer. The supplier monitors the customer's inventory levels, places orders automatically, and ensures that the customer does not run out of product.

Edwards Brothers Malloy
Oxnard, CA USA
April 30, 2014